Mike McGrath

Visual Basic

6th edition

In easy steps is an imprint of In Easy Steps Limited
16 Hamilton Terrace · Holly Walk · Leamington Spa
Warwickshire · United Kingdom · CV32 4LY
www.ineasysteps.com

Sixth Edition

Notice of Liability
Every effort has been made to ensure that this book contains accurate
and current information. However, In Easy Steps Limited and the
author shall not be liable for any loss or damage suffered by readers
as a result of any information contained herein.

Trademarks
All trademarks are acknowledged as belonging to their respective
companies.

In Easy Steps Limited supports The Forest Stewardship Council (FSC),
the leading international forest certification organization. All our titles
that are printed on Greenpeace approved FSC certified paper carry the
FSC logo.

MIX
Paper from
responsible sources
FSC® C020837

Printed and bound in the United Kingdom

ISBN 978-1-84078-872-3

Contents

Preface

The creation of this book has provided me, Mike McGrath, a welcome opportunity to update my previous books on Visual Basic programming with the latest techniques. The examples are created in the latest Visual Studio Community edition development suite, and the book's screenshots illustrate the actual results produced by compiling and executing the listed code.

Conventions in this book

In order to clarify the code listed in the steps given in each example, I have adopted certain colorization conventions that simulate the default syntax highlighting of the Visual Studio code editor. Visual Basic keywords are colored blue; Visual Basic objects are light blue; string values are red; comments are green; and all other code is black – like this:

```
' Create an XMLDocument object from a specified XML file.
Dim doc As New System.Xml.XmlDocument
doc.Load( "C:\Users\Mike\Documents\Books.xml" )
```

Additionally, in order to identify each source code item described in the steps, a colored icon and name appears in the margin alongside the steps:

Visual Basic Project   VBA Word Macro   VBA Excel Macro   VBScript File

Grabbing the source code

For convenience I have placed source code files from the examples featured in this book into a single ZIP archive. You can obtain the complete archive by following these easy steps:

1. Browse to **www.ineasysteps.com** then navigate to Free Resources and choose the Downloads section

2. Find Visual Basic in easy steps, 6th Edition in the list, then click on the hyperlink entitled All Code Examples to download the archive

3. Now, extract the archive contents to any convenient location on your computer

I sincerely hope you enjoy discovering the powerful, expressive possibilities of Visual Basic programming and have as much fun with it as I did in writing this book.

1 Getting started

Welcome to the exciting world of Visual Basic programming. This chapter introduces the Visual Studio Integrated Development Environment (IDE) and shows you how to create a real Windows application.

Introducing Visual Basic

In choosing to start programming with Visual Basic you have made an excellent choice – the Visual Basic programming language offers the easiest way to write programs for Windows. This means you can easily create your own programs to give maximum control over your computer and automate your work to be more productive. Also, programming with Visual Basic is fun!

Like other programming languages, Visual Basic comprises a number of significant "keywords" and a set of syntax rules. Beginners often find its syntax simpler than other programming languages, making Visual Basic a popular first choice to learn.

Although writing programs can be complex, Visual Basic makes it easy to get started. You can choose how far to go. Another advantage of Visual Basic is that it works with Microsoft Office applications and with the Windows Script Host within the Windows operating system – so the possibilities are immense...

- **Visual Basic (VB)** – quite simply the best programming language for the novice or hobbyist to begin creating their own standalone Windows applications, fast.
- **Visual Basic for Applications (VBA)** – an implementation of Visual Basic that is built into Microsoft Office applications. It runs within a host rather than as a standalone application.
- **Visual Basic Script (VBScript)** – a derivative of Visual Basic that can be used for Windows scripting.

The evolution of Visual Basic

- Visual Basic 1.0 released in May 1991 at the Comdex trade show in Atlanta, Georgia, USA.
- Visual Basic 2.0 released in November 1992 – introducing an easier and faster programming environment.
- Visual Basic 3.0 released in the summer of 1993 – introducing the Microsoft Jet Database Engine for database programs.
- Visual Basic 4.0 released in August 1995 – introducing support for controls based on the Component Object Model (COM).
- Visual Basic 5.0 released in February 1997 – introducing the ability to create custom user controls.
- Visual Basic 6.0 released in the summer of 1998 – introducing the ability to create web-based programs. This hugely popular edition is the final version based on COM and is often referred to today as "Classic Visual Basic".
- Visual Basic 7.0 (also known as Visual Basic .NET) released in 2002 – introducing a very different object-oriented language based upon the Microsoft .NET framework. This controversial edition broke backward-compatibility with previous versions, causing a rift in the developer community.
- Visual Basic 8.0 (a.k.a. Visual Basic 2005).
- Visual Basic 9.0 (a.k.a. Visual Basic 2008).
- Visual Basic 10.0 (a.k.a. Visual Basic 2010).
- Visual Basic 11.0 (a.k.a. Visual Basic 2012).
- Visual Basic 12.0 (a.k.a. Visual Basic 2013).
  (Version numbering of Visual Basic skipped 13 to keep in line with the version numbering of Visual Studio itself.)
- Visual Basic 14.0 (a.k.a. Visual Basic 2015).
- Visual Basic 15.0 (a.k.a. Visual Basic 2017).
- Visual Basic 16.0 (a.k.a. Visual Basic 2019).

All examples in this book are created for Visual Basic 16.0 although many of the core language features are common to previous versions of the Visual Basic programming language.

Hot tip

Visual Basic derives from an earlier simple language called BASIC, an acronym –
Beginners
All-purpose
Symbolic
Instruction
Code.
The "Visual" part was added later as many tasks can now be accomplished visually, without actually writing any code.

Installing Visual Studio

In order to create Windows applications with the Visual Basic programming language you will first need to install a Visual Studio Integrated Development Environment (IDE).

Microsoft Visual Studio is the professional development tool that provides a fully Integrated Development Environment for Visual Basic, Visual C++, and Visual C#. Within its IDE, code can be written in C++, C#, or the Visual Basic programming language to create Windows applications.

Visual Studio Community edition is a streamlined version of Visual Studio specially created for those people learning programming. It has a simplified user interface and omits advanced features of the professional edition to avoid confusion. Within its IDE, code can be written in the Visual Basic programming language to create Windows applications.

Both Visual Studio and Visual Studio Community provide a Visual Basic IDE for Visual Basic programming. Unlike the fully-featured Visual Studio product, the Visual Studio Community edition is completely free and can be installed on any system meeting the following minimum requirements:

Visual Studio is used to develop computer programs, web apps, mobile apps, and more.

Component	Requirement
Operating system	Windows 10 (version 1703 or higher) Windows Server 2019 Windows 8.1 (with update 2919355) Windows 7 Service Pack 1 Windows Server 2012 R2
CPU (processor)	1.8 GHz or faster
RAM (memory)	2 GB (8 GB recommended)
HDD (hard drive)	Up to 210 GB available space
Video Card	Minimum resolution of 1280 x 720 Optimum resolution of 1366 x 768

The Visual Studio Community edition is used throughout this book to demonstrate programming with the Visual Basic language, but the examples can also be recreated in Visual Studio. Follow the steps opposite to install Visual Studio Community edition.

1 Open your web browser and navigate to the Visual Studio Community download page – at the time of writing this can be found at **visualstudio.microsoft.com/vs/community**

Installation of Visual Studio is handled by an installer application. You can re-run the installer at a later date to add or remove features.

2 Click a button to select your operating system – **Windows** or **macOS**

3 Now, click on the **Download** button to grab the installer

4 Open your **Downloads** folder, then click on the installer file icon to fetch some setup files

5 Choose the two **VB** options as the type of installation

Choosing a different destination folder may require other paths to be adjusted later – it's simpler to just accept the suggested default.

6 Click the **Install** button to begin the download and installation process

Exploring the IDE

1 Go to your Apps menu, then select the Visual Studio 2019 menu item added there by the installer:

The first time Visual Studio starts it takes a few minutes as it performs configuration routines.

2 Sign in with your Microsoft account, or register an account then sign in, to continue

3 See a default **Start Page** appear where recent projects will be listed alongside several "Get started" options

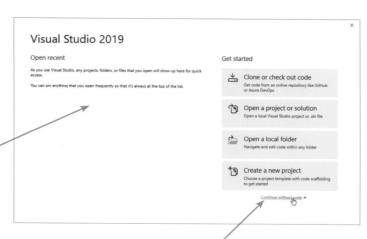

In the future your recent projects will be listed here so you can easily reopen them.

4 For now, just click the link to **Continue without code** to launch the Visual Studio application

The Visual Studio Integrated Development Environment (IDE) appears, from which you have instant access to everything needed to produce complete Windows applications – from here you can create exciting visual interfaces, enter code, compile and execute applications, debug errors, and much more.

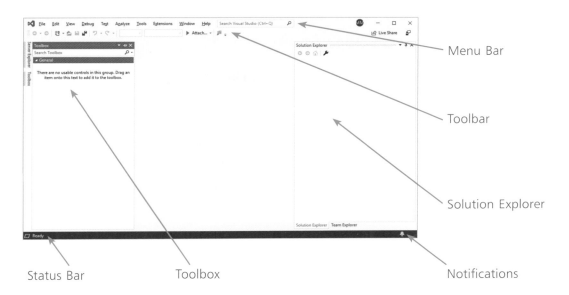

Menu Bar

Toolbar

Solution Explorer

Status Bar

Toolbox

Notifications

Visual Studio IDE components

The Visual Studio IDE initially provides these standard features:

- **Menu Bar** – where you can select actions to perform on all your project files and to access Help. When a project is open, extra menus of Project, and Build, are shown in addition to the default menu selection of File, Edit, View, Debug, Test, Analyze, Tools, Extensions, Window, and Help.

- **Toolbar** – where you can perform the most popular menu actions with just a single click on its associated shortcut icon.

- **Toolbox** – where you can select visual elements to add to a project. Click the Toolbox side bar button to see its contents. When a project is open, "controls" such as Button, Label, CheckBox, RadioButton, and TextBox are shown here.

- **Solution Explorer** – where you can see at a glance all the files and resource components contained within an open project.

- **Status Bar** – where you can read the state of the current activity being undertaken. When building an application a "Build started" message is displayed here, changing to a "Build succeeded" or "Build failed" message upon completion.

Hot tip

To change the color, choose the **Tools**, **Options** menu then select **Environment**, **General, Color Theme**.

13

Starting a new project

GettingStarted

1 On the Menu Bar, click **File**, **New**, **Project** to open the "Create a new project" dialog

2 Next, you must choose "Language", "Platform", and "Project type" – select **Visual Basic**, **Windows**, **Desktop**

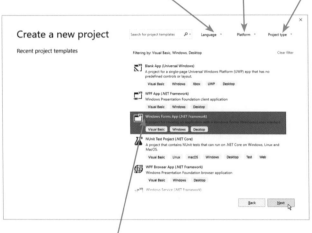

3 Now, select the **Windows Forms App** option

4 Click the **Next** button to open the "Configure your new project" dialog

Hot tip

Leave the **Create directory for solution** option checked to create a folder named as the project name, and located by default in a **C:\Users***username***\ source\repos** directory.

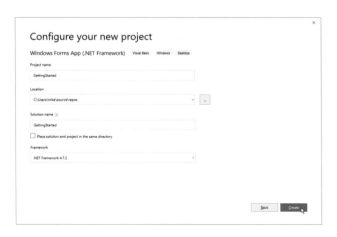

...cont'd

5 Enter a name of your choice in the **Project name** field – in this case, the project name will be "GettingStarted"

6 Click on the **Create** button to create the new project

Visual Studio now creates your new project and loads it into the IDE. A tabbed **Designer** window appears displaying a default empty Form. You can select the **View, Solution Explorer** menu to open a Solution Explorer window that reveals all files in your project, and you can select the **View, Properties Window** menu to open a **Properties** window listing all properties of your Form.

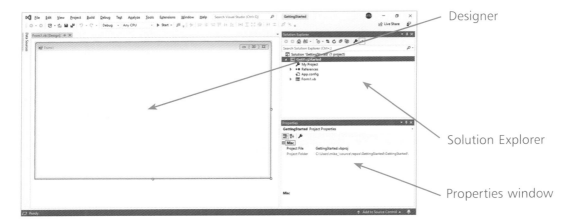

Designer

Solution Explorer

Properties window

The **Designer** is where you create visual interfaces for your applications, and the **Properties** window contains details of the item that is currently selected in the Designer window.

The Visual Studio IDE has now gathered all the resources needed to build a default Windows application – click the **Start** button on the Toolbar to launch this application. The application simply creates a basic window – you can move it, minimize it, maximize

it, resize it, and quit the application by closing it. It may not do much, but you have already created a real Windows program!

Alternatively, you can run applications using the **Debug**, **Start Debugging** menu options.

Adding a visual control

The **Toolbox** in the Visual Studio IDE contains a wide range of visual controls that are the building blocks of your applications. Using the project created on page 15, follow these steps to start using the Toolbox now:

The **Toolbox** will automatically hide when you click on another part of the IDE, but it can be fixed in place so it will never hide, using the 📌 pin button on the Toolbox bar.

1 Click **View**, **Designer** to see the Designer window

2 Next, click **View**, **Toolbox** on the Menu Bar, or click the Toolbox side bar button, to display the Toolbox categories

If no controls are visible in the Toolbox, right-click on the Toolbox then choose **Show All** to reveal the categories.

3 Now, click on the expansion arrow beside the **Common Controls** category heading to expand the list of visual controls. Usefully, each control name appears beside an icon depicting that control as a reminder. You can click on the **Common Controls** category heading again to collapse the list, then expand other categories to explore the range of controls available to build your application interfaces

Any pinned Window in the IDE can be dragged from its usual location to any position you prefer. Drag it back to the initial location to re-dock it.

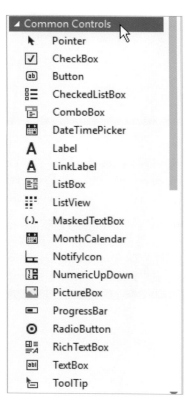

4 Click and drag the **Button** item from the Common Controls categories in the Toolbox onto the Form in the Designer window, or double-click the Button item, to add a Button control to the Form

Hot tip

A **Button** is one of the most useful interface controls – your program determines what happens when the user clicks it.

The Button control appears in the Designer window surrounded by "handles" that can be dragged to resize the button's width and height. Click the ▶ **Start** button to run the application and try out your button.

The Button control behaves in a familiar Windows application manner, with "states" that visually react to the cursor:

Default State

Hover State

Down State

Don't forget

This **Button** control performs no function when it's clicked – until you add some code.

Adding functional code

The Visual Studio IDE automatically generates code, in the background, to incorporate the visual controls you add to your program interface. Additional code can be added manually, using the IDE's integral **Code** editor window, to determine how your program should respond to interface events – such as when the user clicks a button.

Using the project created on page 17, follow these steps to start using the Visual Studio **Code** editor now:

Switch easily between the **Code** window and **Designer** window by clicking on the appropriate window tab.

1   Double-click on the **Button** control you have added to the default Form in the Designer window. A new tabbed text window opens in the IDE – this is the **Code** editor window

2   The cursor is automatically placed at precisely the right point in the code at which to add an instruction to determine what the program should do when this button is clicked. Type this instruction into the **Code** editor **MsgBox("Hello World!")**

This **Solution Explorer** and **Properties** windows are closed here for clarity. You can reopen them at any time from the **View** menu.

3 Click the **Start** button to run the application and test the code you have just written to handle the event that occurs when the button is clicked

Use the **View** menu on the Menu Bar to open the **Code** editor, Form **Designer**, or any other window you require at any time.

4 Push the **OK** button to close the dialog box, then click the **X** button on the Form window, or click the **Stop Debugging** button on the Menu Bar, to stop the program

Each time the button in this application is pressed, the program reads the line of code you added manually to produce a dialog box containing the specified message. The action of pressing the button creates a **Click** event that refers to the associated "event-handler" section of code you added to see how to respond.

In fact, most Windows software works by responding to events in this way. For instance, when you press a key in a word processor a character appears in the document – the **KeyPress** event calls upon its event-handler code to update the text in response.

The process of providing intelligent responses to events in your programs is the very cornerstone of creating Windows applications with Visual Basic.

Saving projects

Even the simplest Visual Basic project comprises multiple files that must each be saved on your system to store the project.

Follow these steps to save the current project to disk:

You can click **File**, **Close Solution** on the Menu Bar to close an open project – a dialog will prompt you to save any changes before closing.

1 Click the **Save All** button on the Toolbar, or click **File**, **Save All** on the Menu Bar, or press **Ctrl + Shift + S**

2 Your project is now saved at its default save location

3 To discover or change the save location, click **Tools** on the Menu Bar, then select the **Options** item – to open the **Options** dialog

4 Expand **Projects and Solutions** in the left-hand pane, then choose the **Locations** option to reveal **Projects location**

Find the **Debug** folder in your saved project directory containing the application's executable (**.exe**) file – you can double-click this to run your program like other Windows applications.

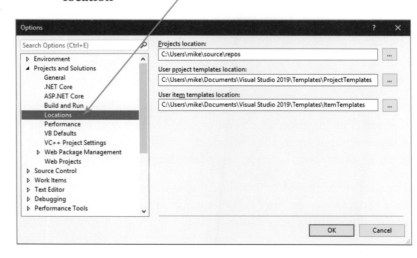

Reopening projects

Use these steps to reopen a saved Visual Basic project:

1 Click **File**, **Open**, **Project/Solution...** on the Menu Bar to launch the **Open Project/Solution** dialog

2 In the **Open Project/Solution** dialog, select the folder containing the project you wish to reopen, and **Open** it

3 Select the Visual Basic Solution file with the extension **.sln** to reopen the project, or open the folder bearing the project name then select the Visual Basic Project File with the extension **.vbproj** to reopen the project

Beware

Only have one project open at any given time to avoid confusion – unless several are needed to be open together for advanced programming.

Hot tip

If you don't see the Designer window after you have reopened a project, click on the **MainWindow.xaml** icon in **Solution Explorer** to make it appear.

Summary

- A project template selected in the **Create a new project** dialog is used to begin a new Windows application project.

- A unique name should be entered into the **Configure your new project** dialog when you create a new Visual Basic project.

- The Form **Designer** window of the Visual Studio IDE is where you create the visual interface for your program.

- Visual controls are added from the **Toolbox** to create the interface layout you want for your program.

- A control can be dragged from the **Toolbox** and dropped onto the Form, or added to the Form with a double-click.

- The **Visual Studio IDE** automatically generates code in the background as you develop your program visually.

- The **Code** editor window of the Visual Studio IDE is where you manually add extra code to your program.

- Double-click on any control in the Form **Designer** to open the **Code** editor window at that control's event-handler code.

- The **Start** button on the Visual Studio Toolbar can be used to run the current project application.

- Pressing a button control in a running application creates a **Click** event within the program.

- Code added to a button's **Click** event-handler determines how your program will respond whenever its Click event occurs.

- Providing intelligent responses to events in your programs is the cornerstone of programming with Visual Basic.

- Remember to explicitly save your working project using the **Save All** button on the Toolbar to avoid accidental loss.

- Select the solution file with the **.sln** extension in your chosen saved project directory to reopen that project.

2 Setting properties

This chapter describes how properties of an application can be changed at "design time", when you are creating the interface, and at "runtime", when the application is actually in use.

Form properties

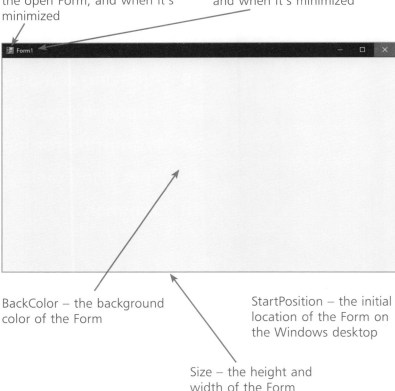

Most applications created with Visual Basic are based upon a window "Form" – a canvas on which to paint the user interface. In some cases, an application will have more than one Form, and Visual Basic lets you display and hide Forms while the application is running. Closing the main Form quits the application.

Like all Visual Basic objects, each Form has several interesting familiar properties, such as those distinguished below.

Icon – a small graphic appearing at the top left-hand corner of the open Form, and when it's minimized

Text – a caption appearing in the title bar of the open Form, and when it's minimized

Form1

BackColor – the background color of the Form

StartPosition – the initial location of the Form on the Windows desktop

Size – the height and width of the Form

A Form is a window. That is why Forms have a Maximize, Minimize and Close button like all other regular windows.

Meeting the properties editor

The Visual Studio IDE provides a **Properties** window where object properties can be inspected. This displays a list of the currently selected object's properties, and their current values. The full list of Form properties, for example, is much larger than the few shown opposite, and can be inspected in the property editor.

1 Identify the Properties window in the IDE – if it's not visible, click **View**, **Properties Window** to open it

2 Click on **File**, **New**, **Project** and create a new **Windows Forms App** using the suggested default name

3 Click on the blank Form in the Designer window to display its properties in the **Properties** window

4 Try out the Properties window buttons, immediately above the properties list, to explore different types of categorized and alphabetical display

5 Use the scroll bar in the Properties window to examine the complete list of Form properties and their present values

Every object in Visual Basic can be given a name – the name of the currently selected object appears in the drop-down list at the top of the **Properties** window. The name can be used to reference an object in Visual Basic programming code.

Although "Form1" is the default value for both **Text** and **(Name)** properties, it is important to recognize that the Text property only sets the Form's caption, whereas the (Name) property is used to reference that Form in Visual Basic programming code.

Editing property values

Changing the properties of a Visual Basic object allows you to determine the appearance of that object. When creating an interface, at design time, an object's **Size** property can be changed by moving its handles to resize it in the Form Designer window – its new dimension values will then appear in the Properties window. More usefully, the value of each single Form and **Control** property can be edited directly in the Properties window.

Editing a Form property value

1 Click on a Form in the Designer window to display its properties in the Properties window

2 Find the **Appearance, Text** property in the Properties window, then double-click in the value column alongside it to highlight the present default "Form1" value

3 Type "New Caption" to specify that as a new value for the **Text** property – the text string appears in the value column as you type

4 Hit **Enter**, or click anywhere else, to apply the new value – it now appears on the Form in the Designer window

Although a new value has been assigned to the Form's **Text** property here, its **(Name)** property still has the default value of "Form1" for reference in Visual Basic programming code.

Editing a Control property value

1 **Click View**, **Toolbox** on the Menu Bar or press **Ctrl + Alt + X**, to open the ToolBox

2 Click and drag the **Label** item from the **Common Controls** category, or double-click on it, to add a Label control to a blank default Form

3 In the Form Designer window, double-click on the Label control to display its present property values in the **Properties** window – this will be "Label1" by default

4 Find the **Common, Content** property in the Properties window, then double-click in the value column alongside it to highlight the present default "Label" value

5 Type "New Label Text" to specify that as a new value for the **Text** property – the text string appears in the value column as you type

6 Hit **Enter**, or click anywhere else, to apply the new value – it now also appears on the Label in the Form Designer

Some properties, such as **Icon**, provide a browse button when you click on their value column, so you can navigate to the location of a local resource to select as the new property value.

Whenever you make changes in the IDE, Visual Basic works in the background to make associated changes to the underlying code.

Coding property values

Use the **Properties** window to set design features such as fonts and layout – only use code to initialize text or color values.

Initialize

28

The Visual Basic **Color** object lets you specify a wide range of colors. Try adding an instruction to set this label's **ForeColor** property to **Color.Red**.

In addition to setting property design values for your application in the **Properties** window, you may also set some text and color values in programming code, so the properties get assigned their initial values (are "initialized") when the Form first loads.

Statements to initialize property values should be placed within the Form's **Load** event-handler. This executes the statements it contains when it is called by the action of the Form loading – just as the **Click** event-handler executes its statements when it is called by the action of a user clicking the **Button**.

Initializing Control properties

1 Click on **File**, **New**, **Project** then create a new **Windows Forms App** and name it "Initialize"

2 Click and drag a **Label** item from the Toolbox's **Common Controls** category, or double-click on it, to add a Label control to a blank default Form

3 In the Form Designer window, double-click anywhere on the default Form to launch the **Code** editor – the cursor is automatically placed in the Form's **Load** event-handler section of code, ready to add statements

4 Type an instruction to set the Label's background color
Label1.BackColor = Color.Yellow

5 On the next line, add an instruction to set the Label's text
Label1.Text = "Initialized Text"

6 Click on the **Start** button to run the application and see that the Label properties initialize with the values you have specified

Initializing Form properties

1 Click the **Stop Debugging** button to halt the Initialize application and return once more to the **Code** editor at the Form's **Load** event-handler section of code

2 Type an instruction to attempt to set the Form's background to blue, then hit **Enter**
`Form1.BackColor = Color.Blue`

3 Notice that a wavy underline now appears beneath this line of code – place the mouse pointer over the red wavy line and read the **ToolTip** message that pops up

```
Form1.BackColor = Color.Blue
    Property My.MyProject.MyForms.Form1 As Form1
    'Form1' cannot refer to itself through its default instance; use 'Me' instead.
```

4 The ToolTip message means you cannot refer to the Form by its name within its own event-handler, so change the instruction to see the wavy underline disappear
`Me.BackColor = Color.Blue`

5 Add an instruction to set the Form's text caption
`Me.Text = "Initialized Caption"`

6 Click on the **Start** button to run the application and see that the Form properties initialize with the values you have specified

You need to hit the **Enter** key after typing each statement so that only one statement appears on each line.

Use the special **Me** keyword in place of the Form's name if you want to address to the Form.

Applying computed values

The **Properties** window and initialization code technique allows the programmer to specify static property values at design time. Creating code to calculate further values from known static values allows your application to compute property values at runtime.

Compute

30

1 Click on **File**, **New**, **Project**, then create a new **Windows Forms App** and name it "Compute"

2 From the ToolBox add six **Label** controls and one **Button** control to the default Form, then drag them into position so the Form looks something like the arrangement below

3 Selecting each item in turn, use the Properties window to change the **Text** property value of the Form, Button, and all Labels, to look like this:

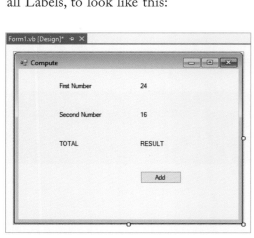

...cont'd

4 To avoid confusion with other controls, use the Properties window to change the **(Name)** property of the three Labels down the right-hand side of the Form to be **Num1**, **Num2**, and **Sum**, reading from top to bottom – the new names can now be used in Visual Basic programming code to refer to these controls

5 Double-click on the **Button** to open the **Code** editor within its **Click** event-handler section of code. Here's where a statement can be added to calculate the total of the static **Text** property values of **Num1** and **Num2**

6 Type a statement assigning the computed total value to the sum Label's **Text** property
Sum.Text = Val(Num1.Text) + Val(Num2.Text)

7 Click on the **Start** button to run the application, then click the button to execute the statement you added and see the **Sum** total value appear

The Visual Basic **Val()** function is used here to extract the numeric version of the text string values so it can perform arithmetic on them – arithmetic functions are fully explained on pages 64-65.

Try adding a further **Button** to provide a clear facility with the statement Sum.Text="" in its Click event-handler.

UserInput

Applying user values

While the Label control works great to display an assigned Text property value, it does not allow the user to directly input a value. The **TextBox** control does both and should be used instead of a Label control where direct dynamic user input is desirable.

Replacing the Label controls named **Num1** and **Num2** in the previous example with TextBox controls of the same name allows the user to dynamically change those values used to compute the sum total value when the **Button** is clicked.

1. Click on **File**, **New**, **Project**, then create a new **Windows Forms App** and name it "UserInput"

2. From the ToolBox add four **Label** controls, two **TextBox** controls, and two **Button** controls to the default Form

3. Use the **Properties** window to change the **Text** property value of the Form, Buttons, and Labels, and arrange their position so the interface looks something like this:

It is good programming practice to give meaningful names to all controls, for easy recognition – the name **AddBtn** makes a Button more easily recognizable than the name **Button1**.

4. To avoid confusion with other controls, use the Properties window to change the **(Name)** property of the two TextBox controls to **Num1** and **Num2**, the Button controls to **BtnAdd** and **BtnClear**, and the Label with the "Result" Text value to **Sum** – the new names can now be used in programming code to refer to these controls

5 Double-click on the **AddBtn** to open the **Code** editor within its Click event-handler, and add the statement
Sum.Text = Val(Num1.Text) + Val(Num2.Text)

6 Double-click on the **ClearBtn** to open the **Code** editor within its Click event-handler, and add the statements
Sum.Text = "RESULT" : Num1.Text = "" : Num2.Text = ""

Multiple statements can be added on a single line if they are separated from each other by a colon character.

7 Click on the **Start** button to run the application. Enter any numeric values you like into the TextBox fields, then click the **AddBtn** button to see the **Sum** total value

UserInput

First Number — 22.5

Second Number — 47.5

TOTAL — 70

Clear   Add

When typing code there is no need to worry about capitals or lowercase letters, as Visual Basic is not case-sensitive.

8 Click the **ClearBtn** button to assign new property values, resuming the application's initial state so that it is ready to add two more input values

Use the **Me** keyword to address the current Form – you can address controls on it by name.

DialogInput

An **InputBox** statement should always contain an = assignment operator to assign the user input to a variable.

Prompting for input

In addition to input via Form window controls, an application can seek user input from an **InputBox** dialog. This is similar to a **MsgBox** dialog but also has a text field where the user can type input that will be returned to the application. The user input value can then be assigned to a property in the usual way.

Unlike a simple code statement that calls up a MsgBox just to advise the user, a statement that calls up an InputBox should make an assignation of the returned value.

1 Click on **File**, **New**, **Project**, then create a new **Windows Forms App** and name it "DialogInput"

2 From the ToolBox, add a **Button** control to the Form

3 Double-click on the Button to open the **Code** editor within its **Click** event-handler, and add the statement **Me.Text = InputBox("Please enter a Caption...")**

4 Click the **Start** button to run the application, then click the Button to call up the InputBox

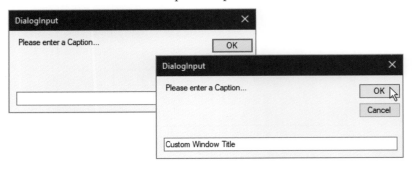

5 Enter any text you like into the input field, then click the **OK** button to assign the value of your input to the Form's **Text** property as a window title caption

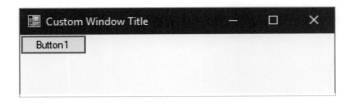

...cont'd

InputBox title and default response

Notice that the **InputBox** title caption assumes the name of the application by default – in this case it's "DialogInput". You may, however, specify your own InputBox title by adding a second string after the message string within the parentheses.

Optionally, you may specify a default response that will appear in the text field when the InputBox is called, by adding a third string within the parentheses. All strings must be separated by a comma.

1 In the DialogInput application, double-click on the **Button** to reopen the **Code** editor within its **Click** event-handler and edit the previous statement to read
Me.**Text** = **InputBox(**"Please enter a Caption..." , _
"Caption Selector" , "Default Window Title" **)**

Notice how the special space + underscore (_) characters are used here to allow the statement to continue on the next line.

2 Click the **Start** button to run the application, then click the Button to call up the InputBox

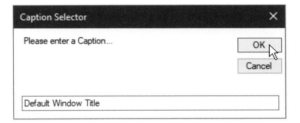

3 Note the InputBox title caption, then click the **OK** button to assign the default response value to the Form's **Text** property as a window title caption

Try specifying a message and a default response – separating the two strings by TWO commas.

Specifying dialog properties

The features of a **MsgBox** dialog can be determined by adding a comma and specification value after the message string within its parentheses. This can specify which buttons the dialog will display and what graphic icon, if any, will appear on the dialog.

Button constant	Value
vbOkOnly	0
vbOkCancel	1
vbAbortRetryIgnore	2
vbYesNoCancel	3
vbYesNo	4
vbRetryCancel	5

The dialog button combinations can be specified using the Visual Basic constant values, or their numeric equivalents, in this table. For example, to have the dialog display Yes, No, and Cancel buttons, specify the **vbYesNoCancel** constant or its numeric equivalent **3**.

Icon constant		Value
vbCritical	✖	16
vbQuestion	?	32
vbExclamation	!	48
vbInformation	i	64

The dialog icon can be specified using the Visual Basic constant values, or their numeric equivalents, in this table. For example, to have the dialog display the question mark icon, specify the **vbQuestion** constant or its numeric equivalent **32**.

Hot tip

Always specify a graphic icon when calling a **MsgBox** dialog to help the user easily understand the nature of the message.

In order to have the **MsgBox** display both a particular button combination and a certain graphic icon, the specification can add the button constant and the icon constant together using the addition + operator. For example, the specification to display Yes, No, and Cancel buttons along with a question icon would be **vbYesNoCancel + vbQuestion**. Alternatively, specify the sum total of their numeric equivalents – in this case it's **35** (3 + 32).

...cont'd

The buttons in a **MsgBox** dialog each return a specific numeric value to the application when they are clicked. This can be assigned to a property in much the same way as the value returned from the **InputBox** dialog in the previous example.

1 Click on **File, New, Project,** then create a new **Windows Forms App** and name it "MsgBoxDialog"

2 From the ToolBox add a **Button**, a **Label**, and a **TextBox** to the default Form and arrange them to your liking

3 Set the Label's **Text** property to "Button Value :" and name the TextBox **TxtValue**

4 Double-click on the **Button** to open the **Code** editor within its **Click** event-handler, and add the statement
TxtValue.Text = MsgBox("Click any button"**, _
vbYesNoCancel + vbQuestion)**

5 Press the **Start** button to run the application, then click any button and note the value it returns to the **TextBox**

MsgBoxDialog

37

Don't confuse the button return values with the Visual Basic constant values used to specify the button combinations.

Try changing the **MsgBox** combination specification using constant or numeric values – and make a note of the value returned by each button.

Summary

- In Visual Basic each object has a name and properties.

- When an object is selected in the Form Designer the current value of each of its properties can be inspected in the **Properties** window.

- The value of any property can be edited in the Properties window to assign a new value to that property.

- Features determining the appearance of an application, such as **Font** and **Layout**, can be set at design time along with content.

- Content such as **Text** and **Color** values can also be initialized at runtime using the Form's **Load** event-handler.

- **Control** objects placed on a Form can be addressed by their name, but you should use the **Me** object name to address the current Form itself.

- Programming code can use existing property values in a calculation to compute a further value at runtime.

- **Label** controls merely display text, they do not allow user input.

- **TextBox** controls both display text and allow user input.

- It is recommended you give all controls a meaningful name for easy recognition.

- Visual Basic is not case-sensitive so no special care is needed to observe capital or lowercase letters in code.

- An **InputBox** allows user input to be assigned to any property.

- Unlike a **MsgBox** statement, a call to the **InputBox** should always assign the value that will be returned.

- Optionally, a title and default response can be specified for an **InputBox** dialog.

- Optionally, a button combination and icon can be specified for a **MsgBox** dialog.

3 Using controls

This chapter illustrates how many of the Common Controls within the Visual Basic Toolbox can be used to develop an exciting application interface.

Tab order

When creating an application interface with multiple controls, consider how it can be navigated without a mouse by those users who prefer keyboard navigation. Typically, they will expect to be able to move the focus from one control to another by pressing the **Tab** key. It is therefore important to allow the focus to move in a logical order when the Tab key is pressed, by setting the **TabIndex** property values of your controls.

TabIndex

1 Place several controls on a Form, then click on the one you want to be first in the **Tab** order to select it

In Windows applications the term "focus" describes which control is active. Pressing the **Enter** key is equivalent to clicking on the control in current focus.

2 Set the **Behavior, TabIndex** property value of the selected control to zero so it has first focus

Not all controls can receive focus. The **Label** controls in this example are not able to get focus, so the tab action just skips to the next control.

3 Repeat for other controls, setting each **TabIndex** with an ascending value – 1, 2, 3, and so on

4 Press the **Start** button to run the program, then hit the Tab key to see the focus follow your chosen order

Using Button

The **Button** control provides the user with an easy way to start an operation, confirm or cancel a choice, or get help. In Visual Basic, programming code needs to be added within each Button's event-handler to determine its function. Also, its properties need to be set to determine its appearance – Size, Text, Color, Font, etc. When setting the **Text** property you can easily create an access key shortcut by prefixing the value with an ampersand **&** character.

1 Select the **Button** control in the Form Designer, then use the **Properties** window to modify its **Size** and **Color**

AccessKey

2 Assign a **Text** property value that is prefixed by an ampersand **&** character to create an access key shortcut

The **Enabled** property can be set to **False** to prevent a Button being available to the user until your program enables it.

3 Add **MsgBox("Going")** code to the button's **Click** event handler, then run the program and press **Alt + G** to test the "Go" button's access key

The standard Windows look is familiar and comfortable for most users – avoid radical customization of your application.

Using TextBox

The **TextBox** control is an essential part of most applications, typically providing a single-line text input area for the user. Greater amounts of text input can be accommodated in a TextBox if its **Multiline** property is set to **True**, and its **ScrollBars** property is set to **Vertical**.

CharacterCounter

1 Place a **TextBox** and a **Button** control onto a Form

2 Select the TextBox and use the **Properties** window to set its **ScrollBars** property to **Vertical**

3 Click on the **Smart Tag** arrowed button over the TextBox, or use the Properties window, to set its **Multiline** property to **True**

Typing a space into a **TextBox** adds a space character.

4 Add this statement to the Button's **Click** event-handler
```
MsgBox("You typed: " & _
Str ( Len ( TextBox1.Text ) ) & " characters" )
```

5 Run the application, type some text into the **TextBox**, then click the **Button** to test the application

The ampersand **&** character is used in this example to concatenate (join) the strings together.

42

Using ComboBox

A **ComboBox** control can be used in place of a TextBox to provide an additional range of text values in a drop-down list. The user can choose one of the listed values to insert into the text field or type into it directly, just like a regular TextBox. The ComboBox provides a user-friendly list of anticipated input, but occupies only the same space as a single-line TextBox.

1 Select the **ComboBox** control and find its **Data, Items** property in the Properties window

2 Click the ellipsis (**...**) button in its value column to launch the **String Collection Editor**

ComboBox

3 Enter a list of alternatives you wish to offer, adding one on each line, then click the **OK** button

You can discover the value selected by the user from the ComboBox's **Text** property.

43

Using Label

A **Label** control is intended to advise the user, and provides a rectangular area that is generally used to provide text information. It can also provide simple rectangular graphics by displaying no text value and setting its **AutoSize** and **BackColor** properties.

GraphicLabels

1 Add three **Label** controls to a Form

2 Select each Label in turn and, in the **Properties** window, set the **Layout, AutoSize** property value to **False**

Hot tip

You can add an outline to a Label using its **BorderStyle** property.

3 Select each Label in turn and, in the **Properties** window, set the **Appearance, BackColor** property value to a color

4 Select each Label in turn and, in the **Properties** window, delete the **Appearance, Text** property value to be blank

Don't forget

You can use the drop-down list in the **Properties** window to select a control to edit.

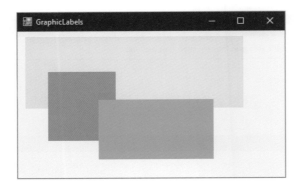

Using PictureBox

The **PictureBox** control allows images to be added to your application interface. These can be referenced as local files or imported into your application as a resource. Adding an image as a resource ensures your application will be portable when deployed, as it includes its own copy of the image.

1 Add a **PictureBox** control to a Form, then select it

2 Find its **Appearance**, **Image** property in the **Properties** window, then click the ellipsis button [...] to launch the **Select Resource** dialog box

3 Check the **Project resource file** radio button, then click **Import** to browse to the location of the image file

4 Click **OK** to import the image file into your application and to place the image in the **PictureBox** control

PictureBox

Beware

Acceptable image formats are Bitmap (**.bmp**), Icon (**.ico**), GIF (**.gif**), Metafile (**.wmf**), and JPEG (**.jpg**).

Hot tip

After importing an image, see the file get added into the **Resources** folder in the **Solution Explorer** window.

Using ListBox

The Visual Basic **ListBox** is one of the most useful controls, as it provides a convenient way to present multiple choices to the user. It allows large lists, of even several thousand items, to be displayed in a compact manner. Typically, the list data is derived from an external source such as a database, then incorporated within your application – address books, business records, collections, etc.

Although the Properties window allows items to be added manually to a ListBox **Items** property, as with a ComboBox, it is often more appropriate to build the list dynamically by adding items at runtime – using the Form's **Load** event-handler.

BookPicker

1   Add a **ListBox**, **Label**, and **Button** control to a Form

2   Name the ListBox "LstBooks" and change the **Text** property values of the Label and Button, like this:

The items in this small list example are added in the code one by one. Larger lists can be added more economically using a code loop – learn more about loops on page 68.

3   Double-click on the Form to open the **Code** editor in the Form's **Load** event-handler and add the statement **LstBooksItems.Add(** "Java in easy steps" **)**

4   Repeat the above statement, each on a new line, substituting a different title within the parentheses for each title you want to add to the list

5 To have the list items sorted alphabetically, add the statement **LstBooks.Sorted = True**

6 To have the first item in the list selected by default, add the statement **LstBooks.SelectedIndex = 0**

Remember that the first item in the index is numbered as zero, not 1.

7 To show the list length in the Form's caption, add the statement **Me.Text = LstBooks.Items.Count & _**
" More Books by Mike McGrath"

8 Return to the Form Designer and double-click on the **Button** to open the **Code** editor in its event-handler. To display the currently selected list item when it is clicked, add the statement **MsgBox(LstBooks.Text)**

You don't need to worry about setting **ListBox** scroll bars for longer lists – they get added automatically.

9 Run the application and see the first item appear selected. Select a different item then click the **Button** to confirm the selection

The ListBox's **Sorted** property can also be set in the Properties window.

Using CheckBox

A **CheckBox** control is a small box with a caption. It lets the user select the caption choice by clicking on the box, and a check mark appears in the box to indicate it has been chosen. Clicking the box once more deselects the choice and unchecks the box.

CheckBox controls are ideal to present a set of choices from which the user can select none, one, or more than one choice.

PizzaPicker

1 Add two **CheckBox** controls to a Form along with a **Label**, **ListBox**, and **Button**

2 Use the **Properties** window to change the **Text** property values of the CheckBox controls, Label, and Button to look like the ones below, and name the ListBox "LstPizza"

Don't forget

The conditional **If-Then** statements shown here are explained in detail on page 66. For now, just remember that the **Checked** property is set to **True** when chosen.

3 Add this statement to the Button's **Click** event-handler to clear the list box when it's clicked **LstPizza.Items.Clear()**

4 Now, add these statements to the Button's **Click** event-handler – to add list items for each checked CheckBox control

```
If CheckBox1.Checked = True Then
        LstPizza.Items.Add( Checkbox1.Text )
End If

If CheckBox2.Checked = True Then
        LstPizza.Items.Add( Checkbox2.Text )
End If
```

Using RadioButton

A **RadioButton** control is like a CheckBox, but with one crucial difference – the user can check only one choice in the group. Checking a RadioButton automatically unchecks any others.

RadioButton controls are ideal to present a set of choices from which the user can select only one choice.

1 Add two **RadioButton** controls and a **Label** to the Form opposite, then edit their **Text** properties to look like this:

When creating **RadioButton** groups, always set one choice as the default by changing its **Checked** property value to **True** in the Properties window.

2 Insert these statements in the Button's **Click** event-handler, straight after the clear instruction

```
If RadioButton1.Checked = True Then
        LstPizza.Items.Add( RadioButton1.Text )
End If

If RadioButton2.Checked = True Then
        LstPizza.Items.Add( RadioButton2.Text )
End If
```

3 Run the application, select various choices, then click the **Button** to test the selection results

Try adding a Clear button to the Form that will clear the **ListBox** and all selected choices when it gets clicked.

Using WebBrowser

The Visual Basic **WebBrowser** control makes it a snap to quickly add a document viewer to your application, which can view HTML documents both online and on your own computer. It can also display plain text and image files – just like your web browser.

SimpleBrowser

1 Add a **WebBrowser** control to a Form – it will automatically occupy the entire Form area

2 Click on the **Smart Tag** arrow button and select the **Undock in Parent Container** link

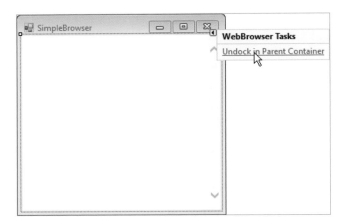

3 Add a **TextBox** and **Button** control, then arrange the Form controls to look like this:

Grab the handles around the controls to resize them on the Form.

4 Double-click on the **Button** to open the **Code** editor in its event-handler, then add the following statement
WebBrowser1.Navigate(TextBox1.Text)

5 Run the application, type a valid URL into the **TextBox** field, then click the **Button** to view the web page

The **Enter** key will not activate the button's **Click** event unless you add an access key shortcut.

6 Type a valid local file address into the **TextBox** field and click the **Button** to view it in the **WebBrowser** control

You can download the projects from this book: visit **www.ineasysteps. com** then navigate to **Free Resources** and choose the **Downloads** section.

Using Timer

The **Timer** is an invisible control that can be found in the **Components** section of the Visual Studio **ToolBox**. When added to your application it fires an event at a regular interval set by you. Statements within the Timer's event-handler are then executed whenever the **Timer** event occurs.

ToggleTimer

Set the **PictureBox** controls to **AutoSize** using the Smart Tags or the Properties window.

Controls can be accidentally repositioned – use **Lock Controls** under the **Format** menu to be sure they stay put.

1 Add two **PictureBox** controls and a **Button** to a Form

2 Assign two similar images of the same size to the **PictureBox** controls, then hold down the **Shift** key while you click on each to select both together

3 On the Menu Bar select **Format, Align, Centers** to exactly align the PictureBox controls one above the other

4 Select **Format, Order, Bring to Front** or **Send to Back** to ensure that PictureBox1 is at the front (on top) of the PictureBox2 control – click on the top one and check the currently selected control name in the **Properties** window

5 Add a **Timer** control to the Form from the **Components** section of the ToolBox – its icon appears on the **Component Tray** at the bottom of the Form Designer

6 Double-click on the Timer icon to open the **Code** editor at its **Tick** event-handler, then add these statements

```
If PictureBox1.Visible = True Then
        PictureBox1.Visible = False
Else
        PictureBox1.Visible = True
End If
```

This code inspects the **Visible** property of the top **PictureBox** and "toggles" its visibility on and off – like flicking a light switch

7 Double-click on the **Button** to open the **Code** editor at its event-handler, then add these statements

```
If Timer1.Enabled = False Then
        Timer1.Enabled = True
Else
        Timer1.Enabled = False
End If
```

This code inspects the **Enabled** property of the **Timer** and "toggles" it on and off when the **Button** gets clicked

8 Run the application, then click the **Button** to watch the Timer appear to animate the PictureBox images

The popular controls demonstrated in this chapter are just some of the many controls available in the **ToolBox** – experiment with each one to understand them.

You can adjust the Timer's **Interval** property value to change the speed of the animation.

53

Summary

- The **TabIndex** property determines the order in which a user can navigate around the interface controls with the **Tab** key.

- Access key shortcuts are assigned to Buttons by prefixing the **Text** property value with an ampersand **&** character.

- **TextBox** controls can usefully display multiple lines of text if their **MultiLine** property is set to **True** and their **ScrollBars** property is set to **Vertical**.

- A **ComboBox** control allows typed text input, like a TextBox, plus it offers the user a list of anticipated input items to click.

- **Label** controls contain text information and do not allow focus or direct input. They can, however, be useful to provide simple rectangular graphics.

- A **PictureBox** control allows an image to be incorporated in the application interface.

- Importing images as a resource ensures that the application will be portable when it is deployed.

- **ListBox** controls are useful to compactly display numerous data items – both from within the program and from external sources such as a database.

- **CheckBox** controls let the user choose none, one, or more options, whereas **RadioButton** controls let the user choose just one option from a group.

- A **WebBrowser** control can display HTML documents plus plain text and images – just like your regular web browser.

- You can use a **Timer** control to create an event in your application that fires at a regular interval set by you.

- The toggle technique is useful in Visual Basic programming to alternate a **Property** value.

4 Learning the language

This chapter demonstrates the mechanics of the Visual Basic programming language, which allow data to be stored, controlled, and manipulated to progress the application.

Elements of a program

A program is simply a series of instructions that tell the computer what to do. Although programs can be complex, each individual instruction is generally simple. The computer starts at the beginning and works through, line by line, until it gets to the end. Here are some of the essential elements in Visual Basic:

Statements

A statement is an instruction that performs an action. For example, the statement **Lbl.BackColor = Color.Blue** sets the background color of **Lbl** to **Blue**.

Functions

A function is a statement that returns a value. For example, the function **InputBox()** returns the value of its dialog text field.

Variables

A variable is a word defined in the program that stores a value. For example, the statement **msg = "Hello World!"** stores a string of characters in a variable called **msg**.

Operators

An operator is an arithmetical symbol. For example, the * asterisk character is the multiplication operator and the / forward slash character is the division operator.

Objects

An object is a program "building block" entity. It can be visible, like a Button control, or invisible, like a Timer control.

Properties

A property is a characteristic of an object. For example, the property **Btn.Text** is the **Text** property of the **Btn** object.

Methods

A method is an action that an object can perform. For example, the method **Btn.Click()** is the **Click** method of the **Btn** object.

Comments

A comment is an explanatory line in the program code starting with an apostrophe ' character. It's not actually read by the compiler but exists to explain the purpose of the code. For example, ' Clear the list. might explain a **Clear** statement.

The examples in this chapter demonstrate the various elements of a program. Refer back here for identification.

The Visual Basic IDE is a safe environment in which to experiment and learn from your mistakes.

...cont'd

The illustration below shows the **Code** editor view of Visual Basic programming code for the **Click** event-handler of a **Button** control – line numbering is turned On to aid analysis of the code.

To turn on line numbering, click on **Tools**, **Options**, then expand **Text Editor**, **Basic**. Choose **General** then check the **Line Numbers** option.

Line-by-line analysis

● Lines 1 and 16 – start and end of the entire Form code.

● Lines 3 and 14 – start and end of the Button event-handler.

● Lines 5, 8, and 11 – explanatory comments.

● Line 6 – creates a variable called **msg** to store String data.

● Line 9 – places text value into the **msg** variable.

● Lines 12 – calls the **MsgBox()** function to show the **msg** value.

Syntax highlighting

● **Keywords** – Visual Basic core language words appear in **blue**.

● **Objects** – Visual Basic objects appear in light blue.

● **Strings** – text values, within double-quotes, appear in red.

● **Comments** – explanatory lines appear in green.

● **Code** – everything else appears in **black**.

The syntax colors shown here are the default colors. Custom colors can be chosen in the **Tools**, **Options** dialog by expanding **Environment**, **Fonts and Colors**.

Declaring variable types

A variable is like a container in a program where a data value can be stored. It is called a variable because its contents can change (vary) during the course of the program.

You can create a variable by typing a declaration comprising the Visual Basic **Dim** keyword followed by a unique variable name of your choice. For example, **Dim msg** declares a new variable with the name **msg**.

The variable declaration should also specify the type of data the variable can store using the **As** keyword followed by one of the Visual Basic data types. So, **Dim msg As String** declares a new variable called **msg** that can store a string of characters.

There are many data types available in Visual Basic programming, but those most frequently used are listed in the table below.

Hot tip

Always choose a meaningful name for your variable to aid its easy recognition.

Data type	Possible value
Boolean	True or False
String	Characters
Integer	Whole number
Double	Floating-point number

After a variable has been created with a specified data type it can only store data of the type specified in the declaration. For example, you cannot assign a **String** to an **Integer** variable.

Data of the appropriate type can be assigned to the variable at any point in the program. A variable declaration can also initialize a variable. For example, **Dim msg As String = "Hello"** initializes a new **String** variable called **msg** with the value **Hello**.

Don't forget

Any value within double quotes is a **String** – so "123" is a **String**, and the content of a **TextBox** is also a **String**.

...cont'd

Specifying data types for variables has several advantages:

- It lets you perform specialized tasks for each data type – character manipulation with **String** values, validation with **Boolean** values, and arithmetic with **Integer** and **Double** values.
- It enables **IntelliSense** to pop up their features as you type.
- It takes advantage of compiler type checking to prevent errors.
- It results in faster execution of your code.

You can easily display the value stored in any variable by assigning it to the text-based property of visual control, such as a ListBox.

1 Add a **ListBox** control and a **Button** control to a Form

2 Double-click on the Button to launch the **Code** editor in its event-handler

3 Add these lines to declare and initialize four variables
```
Dim bool As Boolean = False
Dim str As String = "Some text"
Dim int As Integer = 1000
Dim num As Double = 7.5
```

4 Now, add these lines to display the stored values
```
ListBox1.Items.Add( "bool value is " & bool )
ListBox1.Items.Add( "str value is " & str )
ListBox1.Items.Add( "int value is " & int )
ListBox1.Items.Add( "num value is " & num )
```

5 Run the application and click the **Button** to see the value stored in each variable

VarTypes

59

Understanding variable scope

The accessibility of a variable is known as its "scope", and depends upon where its declaration is made in the program. A variable's scope determines which parts of the program are able to inspect or change the value stored in that variable.

Variables that are declared within a **Sub** routine section of code, such as an event-handler, are only accessible within that routine. Reference to them from outside that routine will result in an error, as they will not be visible from other routines. A variable declared within a **Sub** routine is, therefore, said to have "local" scope – it is only accessible locally within that routine.

Local variables are generally declared with the **Dim** keyword, a given name, and a data type specification. The given name must be unique within its own scope, but can be used again for another local variable of different scope. For example, two different event-handler **Sub** routines may both declare a local variable called **msg**. There is no conflict here as each one is invisible to the other.

Note that the first line of an event-handler begins with the keywords **Private Sub** – meaning it's a **Sub** routine.

VarScope

Visual Basic projects have a compiler setting called **Option Explicit** that can enforce proper variable declaration, as described here – always leave this set to **On** (its default setting) so you will be obliged to declare variables correctly.

1. Add three **Button** controls to a Form

2. Double-click on the first **Button** to open the **Code** editor in its event-handler and add this code
```
Dim msg As String = "Hello from the Button1 Sub"
MsgBox( msg )
```

3. Double-click on the second **Button** and add this code to its event-handler, which also declares a **msg** variable
```
Dim msg As String = "Hello from the Button2 Sub"
MsgBox( msg )
```

4. Run the application and click each **Button** to confirm the value in each **msg** variable is retrieved without conflict

...cont'd

You may often want a variable to be accessible by more than one **Sub** routine in your program, so its declaration will need to be made outside of any **Sub** routine code. It should, instead, appear in the Form declarations section, right after the Form **Class** line at the start of the code. Variables may be declared here with either the **Private** or **Dim** keyword to become accessible throughout the entire Form scope – so any **Sub** routine can reference them.

The Form Declaration section may also contain variable declarations made with the **Public** keyword to be accessible throughout the entire project, including other Form modules. These are known as "global" variables because they are accessible from absolutely anywhere.

Variable names must be unique within their visible scope.

5 In the **Code** editor, type these declarations into the Form declarations section, at the top of the code
Public globalVar As String = "Hello from the Project"
Private formVar As String = "Hello from this Module"

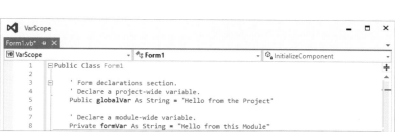

```
     VarScope                                              —  ☐  ×
Form1.vb*  ╫ ×
VB VarScope              ▾  ⚙ Form1              ▾  ⚙ InitializeComponent      ▾
   1  ⊟Public Class Form1                                                     ⊹
   2
   3  ⊟     ' Form declarations section.
   4        ' Declare a project-wide variable.
   5        Public globalVar As String = "Hello from the Project"
   6
   7        ' Declare a module-wide variable.
   8        Private formVar As String = "Hello from this Module"
```

6 Add this line to the third **Button** control's event-handler
MsgBox(globalVar & vbCrLf & formVar)

7 Run the application and click on the third **Button** to retrieve the values from the project-wide and module-wide variables

In deciding where best to declare a variable, always make it as local as possible to avoid errors – your first choice should be a local **Dim** declaration, then a **Private** module declaration, then a **Public** global declaration.

```
     VarScope                           ×

     Hello from the Project
     Hello from this Module


              ╔══════════╗
              ║    OK    ║
              ╚══════════╝
```

VarArray

Working with variable arrays

The variables introduced so far let you store just one value, but sometimes it's more convenient to deal with a set of values. For example, you might want to store the monthly sales figures for a quarterly period. Rather than create three separate variables named **JanSales**, **FebSales**, and **MarSales**, you can create a single variable array named **Sales** with three elements – one for each month. You can refer to them as **Sales(0)**, **Sales(1)**, and **Sales(2)**.

1 Add a **Button** to a Form then create an array variable of three elements in its **Click** event-handler with this code
Dim Sales(2) As Double

2 Assign values to each element in turn
Sales(0) = 5245.00
Sales(1) = 4785.00
Sales(2) = 7365.50

3 Create a regular variable then assign it the total value of all three array elements
Dim Quarter As Double
Quarter = Sales(0) + Sales(1) +Sales(2)

4 Finally, add a statement to display the total value, formatted by the computer's regional currency settings
MsgBox("Quarter Sales:" & FormatCurrency(Quarter))

5 Run the application to test the result. It is shown here producing the total value formatted in dollars, but the formatting depends on the regional settings of the computer on which the application is running

Array indexing begins at zero by default – so the last element of an array of three elements is numbered 2, not 3.

Do not attempt to reference a non-existent array element number in your code. In this example, **Sales(3)** creates an **Out Of Range** error.

You may, if you wish, initialize the array elements in its declaration without explicitly specifying the number of elements. The values should be assigned as a comma-separated list within curly braces. In this example, the declaration would be
Dim Sales() As Double = { 5245.0, 4785.0, 7365.5 }

Multi-dimensional arrays

Arrays can have more than one dimension. For example, you could create a 2-dimensional array to store the monthly sales of two stores over a quarterly period with **Dim Sales(2,1) As Double**. Individual elements can then be referenced as **Sales(0,0)**, **Sales(1,0)**, **Sales(2,0)**, **Sales(0,1)**, **Sales(1,1)**, and **Sales(2,1)**.

1 Add a **Button** to a Form then create an array variable of 3x2 elements in its **Click** event-handler with this code
Dim Sales(2,1) As Double

2 Assign values to each element in turn
Sales(0,0) = 1255 : Sales(1,0) = 1845.5 : Sales(2,0) =1065
Sales(0,1) = 2175 : Sales(1,1) = 2215.5 : Sales(2,1) = 2453

3 Create two regular variables. Assign one the total value of all elements in the array's first dimension, and the other the total value of all elements in its second dimension
Dim Store1, Store2 As Double
Store1 = Sales(0,0) + Sales(1,0) +Sales(2,0)
Store2 = Sales(0,1) + Sales(1,1) +Sales(2,1)

4 Finally, add a statement to display the total values, formatted by the computer's regional currency settings
MsgBox("Quarter Sales..." & vbCrLf & _
"Store 1 : " & FormatCurrency(Store1) & vbCrLf & _
"Store 2 : " & FormatCurrency(Store2))

5 Run the application to test the result. It is shown here producing the total values formatted in dollars, but the formatting depends on the regional settings of the host computer

VarArray ✕

Quarter Sales...
Store1: $4,165.50
Store2: $6,843.50

OK

Arrays of two dimensions represent a square, and those of three dimensions represent a cube, but arrays of more than three dimensions are best avoided as they are difficult to visualize.

63

Notice how the _ underscore character is used here to format the code, and the **vbCrLf** constant is used here to format the MsgBox message **MsgBox** message.

Performing operations

The Visual Basic arithmetic operators listed in the table below are used to return the result of a calculation.

Operator	Description	Example
+	Addition	16 + 4
-	Subtraction	16 - 4
*	Multiplication	16 * 4
/	Division	16 / 4

In statements using more than one arithmetic operator it is important to specify operator precedence to clarify the expression. For example, the expression **6 * 3 + 5** could return 48 (6 * 8) or 23 (18 + 5) – depending which arithmetic is performed first. Adding parentheses around the part to perform first clarifies the expression so that **(6 * 3) + 5** assures the result will be 23 (18 + 5).

The Visual Basic comparison operators listed in the table below are used to test an expression and return a **True** or **False** result.

Operator	Description	Example
=	Equality	num = 10
<>	Inequality	num <> 10
>	Greater than	num > 10
>=	Greater than or equal to	num >= 10
<	Less than	num < 10
<=	Less than or equal to	num <= 10

Beware

In Visual Basic the = symbol is used both to assign values and to test for equality – other programming languages have a separate == equality operator.

The Visual Basic arithmetic operators can be used to easily create simple calculation functionality in your application.

1 Add two **TextBox**, four **Button**, and three **Label** controls to a Form and arrange them as below

SimpleCalculator

2 Double-click on the "Add" button to open the **Code** editor in its event-handler, then type this statement
Label3.Text = "Result : " & _
Str(Val(TextBox1.Text) + Val(TextBox2.Text))

The **&** ampersand character is a Visual Basic operator that is used to concatenate (join) code, and the underscore _ character lets statements continue on the next line.

```
Public Class Form1
    Private Sub Button1_Click(sender As Object, e As EventArgs) Handles Button1.Click

        ' Addition functionality.
        Label3.Text = "Result:  " & Str(Val(TextBox1.Text) + Val(TextBox2.Text))

    End Sub
```

3 Repeat Step 2 for the other **Button** controls but replace the + operator with the appropriate arithmetic operator - for subtraction, / for division, and * for multiplication

4 Run the application and enter two numbers, say 16 and 4, into the **TextBox** fields then click each **Button** control

Branching code

Statements that test an expression allow the program to perform one action or another, according to the result of the test. This important technique is known as "conditional branching" – the code will branch one way or another depending whether a condition is **True** or **False**. In Visual Basic, conditional branching can be performed by an **If** statement, using this syntax:

If (*test-expression-returns-True*) Then
        execute-this-statement
Else
        execute-this-alternative-statement
End If

Optionally, multiple expressions can be included in the test using the **And** keyword, where both expressions must be **True**, or the **Or** keyword where either one of the expressions must be **True**.

Don't forget

If statements always end with **End If** keywords.

IfBranching

1. Add a **Label** control to a Form

2. Double-click on the Form to open the **Code** editor in the Form's **Load** event-handler

3. Type the following **If** statement to assign an appropriate value to the Label control according to whether either of the two tested expressions is **True**
   If (WeekDay(Now) = vbSaturday) Or _
   (WeekDay(Now) = vbSunday) Then
           Label1.Text = "Relax – it's the weekend"
   Else
           Label1.Text = "Today's a working weekday"
   End If

4. Run the application – the message will vary depending on whether the current day is a weekday or a weekend day

Hot tip

If statements were used back on page 53 to toggle property values, and on page 48, without the optional **Else** part, to test the status of **CheckBox** and **RadioButton** controls.

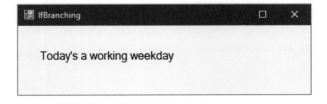

Conditional branching can also be performed with a **Select Case** statement to provide multiple possible branches, using this syntax:

```
Select Case expression-to-test
Case Is test-returns-True
        execute-this-statement-then-exit
Case Is test-returns-True
        execute-this-statement-then-exit
Case Else
        execute-this-default-statement
End Select
```

You can add as many **Case** tests as you wish and, optionally, use **Case Else** to provide a final default statement to be executed when none of the tests return **True**.

1 Add a **Label** control to a Form

2 Double-click on the Form to open the **Code** editor in the Form's **Load** event-handler

3 Type the following statement to assign an appropriate value to the Label control according to which of the tested expressions is true
```
Select Case WeekDay( Now )
Case Is = vbSaturday
        Label1.text = "It's a Super Saturday"
Case Is = vbSunday
        Label1.Text = "It's a Lazy Sunday"
Case Else
        Label1.text = "It's just another working day"
End Select
```

4 Run the application to see an appropriate message

Hot tip

Try using a **Select Case** statement to branch code according to the value returned from a **MsgBox** dialog with Yes, No, and Cancel buttons – as seen on pages 36-37.

SelectBranching

67

Beware

An **If** statement must always end with **End If** keywords, and a **Select Case** statement with the **End Select** keywords.

Looping code

Programming loops allow statements within the loop to be executed repeatedly until the loop ends. They must always include a test expression to determine when to end – or they will run forever! The most popular loop in Visual Basic is the **For Next** loop, which uses a counter to test the number of times it has executed (iterated) its statements, and has this syntax:

For *counter* = *start* To *end*
        execute-this-statement
Next *update-the-counter*

It is often useful to incorporate the increasing value of the counter into the statement/s executed on each iteration of the loop.

ForNextLoop

1   Add a **TextBox**, **Button**, and **ListBox** control to a Form

2   Double-click on the Button to open the **Code** editor in its **Click** event-handler, then type this loop

```
Dim amount As Double = Val( TextBox1.Text )
Dim counter As Integer
For counter = 1 To 10
        ListBox1.Items.Add( "At " & counter & _
        "% interest is " & _
        FormatCurrency( (amount * counter) / 100 ) )
Next counter
```

3   Run the application, enter a number in the **TextBox**, then click the **Button** to run the loop

The counter variable stores the loop index – do not assign it any other value in the loop.

68

...cont'd

Other types of loop possible in Visual Basic are the **Do Until** loop and the **Do While** loop. Although similar, these two loops are subtly different – a **Do Until** loop executes its statements until the test expression becomes **True**, whereas the **Do While** loop executes its statements until the test expression becomes **False**.

All loops work well to iterate over lists of data, and are especially useful to iterate over the values contained in array elements.

1 Add a **ListBox** control to a Form

2 Double-click on the Form to open the **Code** editor in the **Load** event-handler, then create this array
```
Dim Sales() As Double = { 5601, 8502, 6703, 4204, _
7605, 8206, 9107, 6508, 7209, 5010, 8011, 7012 }
```

3 Create a **String** variable with **Dim sum As String**

4 Now, type this loop, then run the application
```
Dim counter As Integer
Do Until counter = Sales.Length
        sum = FormatCurrency( Sales( counter ) )
        counter = counter + 1
        sum = sum & vbTab & MonthName( counter )
        ListBox1.Items.Add( sum )
Loop
```

DoUntilLoop

Choose the **Do** loop, which offers greater clarity for your particular purpose – but remember they must both contain a statement to change the counter, and end with the **Loop** keyword.

The limit of this loop is specified by the **Length** property of the array. The counter references each element (0-11) from the **Sales** array and also each month name (1-12) from the Visual Basic **MonthName** function.

Calling object methods

Visual Basic objects have methods that can be called in code to make the object perform an action at runtime in response to an "event" created by the user. This works in much the same way that you can write code to assign property values to dynamically change an object's characteristics.

To view any object's available properties and methods, type its name followed by a period into the **Code** editor. An "IntelliSense" pop-up window will appear showing all that object's properties and methods. Scroll down the list, then double-click on an item to add that property or method into the code.

CallMethods

1 Add two **Label** and five **Button** controls to a Form

2 In the **Properties** window, set each Label's **Layout**, **AutoSize** to **False**, and delete their default **Text** value

3 Make the **BackColor** of one Label red and name it **LblRed**, then set the other Label's **BackColor** to yellow

4 Edit the **Text** property of each **Button**, then arrange the controls so the Form looks like this:

Leaving the **AutoSize** property set to the default of **True** prevents the **Label** being resized.

5 Double-click on the "Set Bounds" Button to open the **Code** editor in its event-handler, then type **LblRed**.

...cont'd

6 Find the **SetBounds** method in the **IntelliSense** window, then double-click it to add it to the code

7 The **SetBounds** method sets the size and position of the control using X, Y, Width, and Height. Add the settings (**45, 45, 45, 100**) to the code, right after the method name

8 Repeat for the other **Button** controls, adding calls to the **Hide()**, **Show()**, **BringToFront()**, and **SendToBack()** methods – no settings are required for any of these

9 Run the application and click each **Button** to try its action – see the stacking order change from back to front

When you select an item in the **IntelliSense** window a Tooltip appears containing that item's definition.

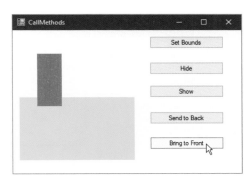

Using the With block shorthand

When creating code addressing several properties or methods of an object it can be tedious to repeatedly type the object name.

```
LblBlue.AutoSize = False
LblBlue.BackColor = Color.Blue
LblBlue.Width = 50
LblBlue.Height = 50
LblBlue.SendtoBack()
```

Usefully, a **With** block can neatly specify all the values and calls:

```
With LblBlue
        .AutoSize = False
        .BackColor = Color.Blue
        .Width = 50
        .Height = 50
        .SendToBack()
End With
```

Try adding another **Label** to this example, then set its properties and methods in the Form's **Load** event using a **With** block.

Creating a sub method

When you double-click on a **Form** or **Button** to open the **Code** editor you see that each event-handler begins and ends like this:

Private Sub ... End Sub

"Sub" is short for "subroutine" and each event-handler subroutine is a **Private** method of that Form's **Class**. You can create your own subroutine method from scratch, which can be called from other code in your application as required.

All executable code must be contained inside a procedure, such as a **Sub** routine or a **Function**.

SubMethod

If you find yourself writing similar code at several points in your application, consider creating a **Sub** routine to make your code more efficient and easier to maintain.

1   Add **Label**, **Button**, and **TextBox** controls to a Form, then arrange them like this:

2   Click on **View, Code** to open the **Code** editor, then type this code into the declarations section
```
Private Sub ClearForm()
        TextBox1.Text = ""
        TextBox2.Text = ""
        TextBox3.Text = ""
End Sub
```

3   Click on **View, Designer** to return to the Form **Designer**, then double-click on the "Clear" **Button** to open the **Code** editor in its **Click** event-handler

4   Type Me. and notice that the new **ClearForm** method has been added to the **IntelliSense** window. Double-click on it to add Me.**ClearForm()** to the code

5   Run the application, type some text into all three text fields, then click the "Clear" **Button** to clear the fields

Sending parameters

A powerful feature of **Sub** routines is the ability to receive information as they are called. This information is known as "parameters" and is sent from the ( ) parentheses of the calling statement to the parentheses of the **Sub** routine.

In order for a **Sub** routine to handle parameters it must specify a name and data type for each parameter it is to receive. For example, **seq As String** would receive a single string parameter from the caller – it cannot be called unless one string is passed. The **Sub** routine code can then refer to the passed value using the given name; in this case, **seq**. Multiple parameters can be passed if the **Sub** routine specifies the correct number and data types.

You can make a **Sub** routine accessible globally by changing its access modifier from **Private** to **Public**.

1 Click **Stop Debugging** to return to the Form window shown opposite

2 Now, click on **View, Code** to open the **Code** editor, then type this code into the declarations section
```
Private Sub Customer(name As String, addr As String)
    TextBox1.Text = name
    TextBox2.Text = addr
End Sub
```

3 Edit the "Customer" **Button** control's **Click** event-handler to include this call to the new **Sub** routine
```
Me.Customer( "Mike McGrath", "1 Main Street, USA" )
```

4 Run the application and click the "Customer" **Button**

Try adding a third parameter to set the "Phone" number field.

Creating a function

A **Function** is similar to a **Sub** routine, but with one important difference – a **Function** returns a value to the caller. This means that you must specify the data type of the return value, in addition to specifying parameters, when creating a **Function**.

ConverterFunction

Hot tip

You can store useful Functions in a code "module". This is an individual file that can be re-used in other projects – effectively extending the Visual Basic language. Click **Project**, **Add Module...** on the Menu Bar to add a new empty code module, or click **Project**, **Add Existing Item...** to add a module created earlier.

Create a **Function** when you need a return value – create a **Sub** routine when no return value is needed.

1 Add a **Button**, a **TextBox**, and three **Label** controls to a Form, then arrange them like this:

2 Click on **View, Code** to open the **Code** editor, then type this code into the declarations section

```
Private Function Inches(ByVal Cm As String) As Double
        Inches = Cm / 2.54
        Inches = FormatNumber( Inches , 2 )
        Return Inches
End Function
```

The parentheses specify that the parameter **Cm** must be a **String** data type – this value is used in the calculation. The result is assigned to the **Function** name for return as a **Double** data type, formatted to just two decimal places.

3 Add a call to the "Inches" **Function** in the Button's **Click** event-handler **Sub** routine

```
Label1.Text = Inches(TextBox1.Text) & " Inches"
```

4 Run the application, enter a number, then click the **Button** to use the **Function**

Doing mathematics

The Visual Basic Math object has many methods that are useful when performing mathematical calculations. The most frequently used methods are listed below, together with examples returns.

Data type	Description
Math.Ceiling()	Rounds a number up; e.g. Math.Ceiling(3.5) returns 4
Math.Floor()	Rounds a number down; e.g. Math.Floor(3.5) returns 3
Math.Round()	Rounds to the nearest integer; e.g. Math.Round(3.5) returns 4
Math.Sqrt()	Returns the square root; e.g. Math.Sqrt(16) returns 4
Math.Max()	Returns the larger of two numbers, e.g. Math.Max(8, 64) returns 64
Math.Min()	Returns the smaller of two numbers, e.g. Math.Min(8, 64) returns 8
Math.Pow()	Returns a number raised to the specified power; e.g. Math.Pow(5, 2) returns 25
Math.Abs()	Returns an absolute value; e.g. Math.Abs(-10.0) returns 10
Math.Cos()	Returns a cosine value; e.g. Math.Cos(10.0) returns -0.839
Math.Log()	Returns a natural logarithm; e.g. Math.Log(10.0) returns 2.303
Math.Sin()	Returns a sine value; e.g. Math.Sin(10.0) returns -0.544
Math.Tan()	Returns a tangent value; e.g. Math.Tan(10.0) returns 0.648

Hot tip

The Math class also has a Math.PI constant representing the value of π – approximately 3.142.

Don't forget

The returns shown here for **Cosine**, **Log**, **Sine**, and **Tangent** are rounded to three decimal places – the actual returns provide greater precision.

Generating a random number

Random numbers can be generated by the Visual Basic **Rnd()** function that returns a floating-point value between 0.0 and 1.0. Multiplying the random numbers will specify a wider range. For example, a multiplier of 20 will create a random number between 0 and 20. To make the generated random number more useful, you can round it up to the nearest higher integer value with the Math. **Ceiling()** method so the range, in this case, becomes from 1 to 20.

The numbers generated by **Rnd()** are not truly random, but are merely a sequence of pseudo random numbers produced by an algorithm from a specific starting point. Whenever an application loads, a call to the **Rnd()** function will begin at the same starting point – so the same sequence will be repeated. This is not generally desirable, so the application needs to create a new starting point when it loads to avoid repetition. This can be achieved by calling the **Randomize()** function in the Form's **Load** event to "seed" the **Rnd()** function with a starting point based upon the system time when the application gets loaded – now the sequence of generated numbers is different each time.

Beware

The numbers generated by the algorithm for **Randomize()** and **Rnd()** may be predicted, so this technique should not be used for cryptography.

RandomGenerator

76

1 Add a **Label**, **TextBox**, and **Button** control to a Form, and arrange them like this:

2 Name the **Label** control **LblMsg**, set its **AutoSize** property to **False**, then assign the text illustrated above to its Text property

3 Name the **TextBox** control **TxtGuess** and set the **Text** property of the **Button** likewise

4 Click on **View, Code** to open the **Code** editor, then create a variable in the Declarations
Dim num As Integer

Don't forget

Text in a **Label** will not wrap to the next line unless **AutoSize** is **False**.

5 Still in the declarations section, add a **Sub** routine to assign a random number 1-20 to the **num** variable

```
Private Sub GetNumber()
        num = Math.Ceiling( Rnd() * 20 )
End Sub
```

6 In the Form's **Load** event-handler add a call to seed the random number generator and a call to set the **num** variable with an initial pseudo random value

```
Randomize()
GetNumber()
```

7 Now, add some logic to the **Button** control's **Click** event-handler with this code

```
Select Case ( Val( TxtGuess.Text) )
Case Is > num
        LblMsg.text = TxtGuess.Text & " is too high"
Case Is < num
        LblMsg.Text = TxtGuess.Text & " is too low"
Case Is = num
        LblMsg.Text = TxtGuess.Text & " is correct" & _
        "I have thought of another number - Try again!"
        GetNumber()
End Select
TxtGuess.Text = ""
```

The integer value must be extracted from the **TextBox** by the **Val()** function before making any comparison.

8 Run the application and guess the random number

You can use the **vbCrLf** constant to format the contents of the **Label**.

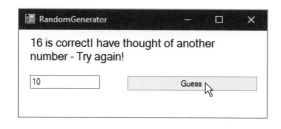

Summary

- A program's essential elements are Statements, Variables, Functions, Operators, object Properties, and object Methods.

- Comment lines help to explain the purpose of the code.

- Variable declarations create a variable and can begin with the **Dim, Public,** or **Private** keywords.

- Each variable declaration should specify the type of data that variable may contain with the **As** keyword and a data type.

- **String, Integer, Double,** and **Boolean** are common data types.

- Numbers can be extracted from a **String** by the **Str()** function, and a **String** converted to a number with the **Val()** function.

- The **Private** and **Dim** keywords allow local scope – where the variable is only accessible within a procedure or module.

- The **Public** keyword allows global scope – where the variable is accessible across an entire program.

- A variable array stores values in elements numbered from zero.

- Operators are used to perform arithmetic and comparison.

- Code can be made to conditionally branch using **If Else** statements or **Select Case** statements.

- **For Next** and **Do Until** statements perform code loops.

- Object properties and methods can be addressed in code.

- A **Function** returns a value but a **Sub** does not.

- Values can be sent to a **Sub** routine or a **Function** if they are of the correct data type and of the number specified.

- The Math object provides many useful methods for performing mathematical calculations.

- Pseudo random numbers can be generated by the **Rnd()** function when seeded by the **Randomize()** function.

5 Building an application

This chapter brings together elements from previous chapters to build a complete application – from the initial planning stage to its final deployment.

The program plan

When creating a new application it is useful to spend some time planning its design. Clearly define the program's precise purpose, decide what application functionality will be required, then decide what interface components will be needed.

A plan for a simple application to pick numbers for a lottery entry might look like this:

Program purpose

● The program will generate a series of six different random numbers in the range 1-59, and have the ability to be reset.

Functionality required

● An initial call to start the random number generator.

● A routine to generate and display six different random numbers.

● A routine to clear the last series from display.

Components needed

● Six **Label** controls to display the series of numbers – one number per Label.

● One **Button** control to generate and display the numbers in the Label controls when this Button is clicked. This Button will not be enabled when numbers are on display.

● One **Button** control to clear the numbers on display in the Label controls when this Button is clicked. This Button will not be enabled when no numbers are on display.

● One **PictureBox** control to display a static image – just to enhance the appearance of the interface.

Omission of the planning stage can result in time-consuming changes to be made later. It's better to "plan your work, then work your plan".

Toggle the value of a Button's **Enabled** property to steer the user. In this case the application must be reset before a further series of numbers can be generated.

...cont'd

Having established a program plan means you can now create the
application basics by adding the components needed to a Form.

1 Open the Visual Studio IDE and create a new Visual
Basic **Windows Forms App** project called "Lotto"

Lotto

2 In the **Form Designer**, add six **Label** controls to the
Form from the **Toolbox**

3 Now, add two **Button** controls and a **PictureBox** control
to the Form

You can drag and drop
items from the **Toolbox**
or double-click them to
add them to the Form.

Assigning static properties

Having created the application basics, as shown on page 81, you can now assign static values using the **Properties** window.

Lotto (cont'd)

You can open the **Properties** window using the **F4** key, or by clicking **View**, **Properties Window** on the Menu Bar.

The Label controls in this program will have their Text property values assigned dynamically at runtime – no static properties are required.

1 Click anywhere on the Form to select it, then in the **Properties** window set the Form's **Text** property to "Lotto Number Picker"

2 Select the first **Button** control, then in the **Properties** window change its **Design, (Name)** property to **BtnPick** and its **Text** property to "Get My Lucky Numbers"

3 Select the second **Button** control, then in the **Properties** window change its **Design, (Name)** property to **BtnReset** and its **Text** property to "Reset"

4 Select the **PictureBox** control, then in the **Properties** window click the **Appearance**, **Image** property ellipsis button to launch the **Select Resources** dialog

5 Click the **Import** button, browse to the image location, then click **OK** to import the image resource – this action automatically assigns it to the PictureBox's **Image** property

Designing the interface

Having assigned static property values, as shown on page 83, you can now design the interface layout.

The size of both the **PictureBox** control and the BtnPick control first needs to be adjusted to accommodate their content. This can easily be achieved by specifying an **AutoSize** value so that Visual Basic will automatically fit the control neatly around its content.

Alternatively, you can use the **Smart Tag** arrow button on a **PictureBox** control to set its **SizeMode** property.

Lotto (cont'd)

1 Select the **PictureBox** control, then in the **Properties** window change its **SizeMode** property to **AutoSize**

2 Select the BtnPick control, then in the **Properties** window set its **AutoSize** property to **True**

Now, you can use the Form Designer's **Format** menu and **Snap Lines** to arrange the interface components to your liking.

Ensure that all PictureBox **Margin** properties are set to zero if you do not require margins around the image.

3 Hold down the left mouse button and drag around the Labels to select all **Label** controls.

4   Click **Format, Align Tops** on the Menu Bar to stack the Labels into a pile

5   Click **Format, Horizontal Spacing, Make Equal** to arrange the pile of Labels into a row

In this case it does not matter in what order the Labels appear in the row.

6   Use the Form's right grab handle to extend its width to accommodate the row of Labels and **PictureBox**, then drag the row and both Buttons to the top-right of the Form

7   Drag the **PictureBox** control to the top-left of the Form, then use the Form's bottom grab handle to adjust its height to match that of the image

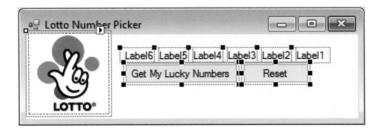

8   Use the **Snap Lines** that appear when you drag controls around the Form to position the row of Labels and the Buttons to make the interface look like this:

Set the Form's **MaximizeBox** property to **False** if you do not wish to have **Maximize** and **Minimize** buttons on the interface.

Initializing dynamic properties

Having designed the interface, as shown on pages 84-85, you can now add some functionality to dynamically set the initial **Text** properties of the **Label** controls and the initial **Button** states.

Lotto (cont'd)

1 Click **View**, **Code** on the Menu Bar to open the **Code** editor window

2 Type the following code into the declarations section, then hit the **Enter** key
Private Sub Clear

The Visual Studio IDE recognizes that you want to create a new subroutine called **Clear**. It automatically adds parameter parentheses after the **Sub** name, and an **End Sub** line to create a subroutine code block.

3 With the cursor inside the new subroutine code block, press **Ctrl + J**, to open the **IntelliSense** pop-up window

4 Scroll down the list of items in the **IntelliSense** window and double-click on the "Label1" item to add it into the **Clear** subroutine code block

The technique described here demonstrates how to use **IntelliSense** – but you can, of course, just type the code directly.

5 Type a period, then double-click the "Text" item when the **IntelliSense** window reappears, to add that code

...cont'd

6 Now, type = "..." to complete the line so it reads like this:
Label1.Text = "..."

7 Repeat this procedure for the other **Label** controls – so that the **Clear** subroutine assigns each an ellipsis string

8 With the cursor inside the **Clear** subroutine code block use **IntelliSense** in the same way to add these two lines
BtnPick.Enabled = True
BtnReset.Enabled = False

This completes the **Clear** subroutine functionality by setting the **Button** states. All that remains is to add a call to the **Clear** subroutine to execute all its instructions when the program starts.

9 In the **Form Designer**, double-click on the Form to open the **Code** editor in its **Load** event-handler, then press **Ctrl + J** to open the **IntelliSense** window

10 Scroll down the list in the **IntelliSense** window and double-click on the "Clear" item you have just created

Hot tip

Add some line breaks and comments to make the code more friendly.

Adding runtime functionality

Having created code to initialize dynamic properties, as shown on pages 86-87, you can now add runtime functionality to respond to clicks on the **Button** controls.

Lotto (cont'd)

1 In the Form **Designer**, double-click on the **BtnReset Button** control to open the **Code** editor in its **Click** event-handler, then add this call to the subroutine **Clear()**

This is all that is needed to provide dynamic functionality for the **BtnReset** control. The main dynamic functionality of this application is provided by the **BtnPick** control, which requires the random number generator to be started when the program starts.

2 In the Form **Designer**, double-click on the Form to open the **Code** editor in its **Load** event-handler, then add this code to start the random number generator **Randomize()**

Now, you can create the code to provide dynamic functionality for the **BtnPick** control itself.

3 In the Form **Designer**, double-click on the **BtnPick Button** control to open the **Code** editor in its **Click** event-handler, then add this line to declare some variables **Dim i, r, temp, nums(60) As Integer**

Don't forget

You don't need to understand in detail the algorithm that is used to shuffle the values.

4 Add a loop to fill the **nums** array elements 1-59 with the integer values 1 to 59
```
For i = 1 To 59
        nums(i) = i
Next
```

5 Add a second loop to shuffle the values within **nums** elements 1-59 – an algorithm to randomize their order
```
For i = 1 To 59
        r = Int(59 * Rnd()) + 1
        temp = nums(i)
        nums(i) = nums(r)
        nums(r) = temp
Next
```

...cont'd

6 Now, add the following lines to display the integer values contained in **nums** elements 1-6 in the **Label** controls
```
Label1.Text = nums(1)
Label2.Text = nums(2)
Label3.Text = nums(3)
Label4.Text = nums(4)
Label5.Text = nums(5)
Label6.Text = nums(6)
```

7 Finally, add these two lines to set the **Button** states ready to reset the application
```
BtnPick.Enabled = False
BtnReset.Enabled = True
```

The variable declaration creates integer variables called "i", "r", and "temp", along with an integer array called "nums" of 60 elements. Element **nums(0)** is not actually used, though.

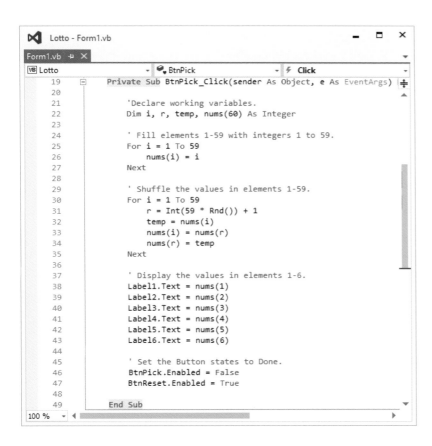

```
Lotto - Form1.vb                                              _  □  ×
Form1.vb  ⊕ ✕
VB Lotto              ▼  🔧 BtnPick        ▼  ⚡ Click           ▼
  19  ⊟       Private Sub BtnPick_Click(sender As Object, e As EventArgs) ⊕
  20
  21              'Declare working variables.
  22              Dim i, r, temp, nums(60) As Integer
  23
  24              ' Fill elements 1-59 with integers 1 to 59.
  25              For i = 1 To 59
  26                  nums(i) = i
  27              Next
  28
  29              ' Shuffle the values in elements 1-59.
  30              For i = 1 To 59
  31                  r = Int(59 * Rnd()) + 1
  32                  temp = nums(i)
  33                  nums(i) = nums(r)
  34                  nums(r) = temp
  35              Next
  36
  37              ' Display the values in elements 1-6.
  38              Label1.Text = nums(1)
  39              Label2.Text = nums(2)
  40              Label3.Text = nums(3)
  41              Label4.Text = nums(4)
  42              Label5.Text = nums(5)
  43              Label6.Text = nums(6)
  44
  45              ' Set the Button states to Done.
  46              BtnPick.Enabled = False
  47              BtnReset.Enabled = True
  48
  49          End Sub
100 % ▼ ◀
```

69

Add comments and line breaks like these to clarify the intention of your code when read by someone else – or when you revisit the code later.

Lotto (cont'd)

Testing the program

Having worked through the program plan, as shown on pages 81-89, the components needed and functionality required have now been added to the application – so it's ready to be tested.

1 Click the **Start** button to run the application and examine its initial start-up appearance

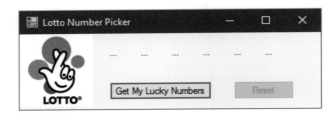

The Form's **Load** event-handler has set the initial dynamic values of each **Label** control and disabled the reset button as required.

2 Click the **BtnPick Button** control to execute the instructions within its **Click** event-handler

A series of numbers within the desired range is displayed, and the **Button** states have changed as required – a further series of numbers cannot be generated until the application has been reset.

3 Make a note of the numbers generated in this first series for comparison later

4 Click the **BtnReset** control to execute the instructions within that **Click** event-handler and see the application return to its initial start-up appearance as required

Notice that no number is repeated in any series.

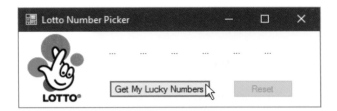

5 Click the **BtnPick Button** control again to execute its **Click** event-handler code a second time

Another series of numbers within the desired range is displayed, and are different to those in the first series when compared – good, the numbers are being randomized as required.

6 Click the **Stop Debugging** button then the **Start** button to restart the application, and click the **BtnPick Button** control once more

The generated numbers in this first series of numbers are different to those noted in the first series the last time the application ran – great, the random number generator is not repeating the same sequence of number series each time the application runs.

Failing to call the **Randomize()** method to seed the Random Number Generator will cause the application to repeat the same sequence each time it runs.

Deploying the application

Having satisfactorily tested the application, as shown on pages 90-91, you can now create a stand-alone version that can be executed outside the Visual Studio IDE and that can be distributed to others for deployment elsewhere.

Lotto (cont'd)

1 Click **Project** on the Menu Bar, choose **Lotto Properties**, **Signing**, then select a signature certificate or simply uncheck the **Sign the ClickOnce manifests** box

Hot tip

Signing applications is optional but does verify authentication. Find more details on ClickOnce at **docs. microsoft.com/ en-us/visualstudio/ deployment/ clickonce-security-and- deployment**

2 Click **Build**, **Build Lotto**, then click **Build**, **Publish Lotto** to launch the **Publish Wizard** dialog

3 Use the wizard's **Browse** button to select a location where you wish to publish the application – the chosen location shown here is the root directory of removable drive **F:**

Hot tip

When choosing a publish location, use the **Create New Folder** button in the **File System** dialog to make a folder to contain all the application files.

4 Click the **Next** button, then select whether the user will install the application from a website, network, or portable media such as CD, DVD, or removable drive – in this case, accept the default portable media option

5 Click the **Next** button, then select whether the installer should check for application updates – accept the default option not to check for updates in this case

6 Click the **Next** button to move to the final dialog page, confirm the listed choices, then click the **Finish** button to publish the application at the specified location

Each time you publish an application, its version number is automatically incremented – 1.0.0.0, 1.0.0.1, 1.0.0.2, etc.

The **Publish Wizard** generates a number of files including a familiar "setup.exe" executable installer.

7 Move the portable media to the system where it is to be deployed, then run **setup.exe** to install the application

When the application is installed on the client system, a shortcut is automatically added to the **Start Menu**, which can be used to launch the application. The user can then run the release version of the application just as it performed during testing of its debug version in the Visual Studio IDE.

An application cannot be published unless it has been built first.

The installer also adds an item to the client system's **Add/Remove Programs** list, which can be used to uninstall the application – just like any other Windows program.

Summary

- Always make an initial program plan to avoid the need for time-consuming changes later.

- A program plan should clearly define the program purpose, functionality required, and components needed.

- Static properties, that will not change when the application is running, can be set at design time in the **Properties** Window.

- An **AutoSize** property value makes Visual Basic automatically fit a control neatly around its content.

- The Form Designer's **Format** menu contains useful features to quickly align and space multiple interface controls.

- **Snap Lines** help you to easily align a selected control to others in the interface at design time.

- Dynamic properties, that will change when the application is running, can be initialized with the Form's **Load** event-handler.

- The pop-up **IntelliSense** window lets you easily add program code when using the **Code** editor.

- Runtime functionality responds to user actions by changing dynamic properties.

- A **Debug** version of an application allows its functionality to be tested as the application is being created in text format.

- The **Build** process compiles a **Release** version of an application in binary format.

- The **Publish** process creates a final **Release** version with an installer so the application can be deployed elsewhere.

- Applications created with the Visual Studio IDE can be installed and uninstalled just like other Windows applications.

6 Solving problems

This chapter describes how to fix errors, debug code, handle exceptions, and get assistance from the Visual Studio Help system.

Real-time error detection

As you type code in the **Code** editor window, the Visual Studio IDE is constantly monitoring your code for possible errors. When you hit the **Enter** key at the end of each line it examines the line you have just typed, and provides real-time feedback of possible errors by adding a wavy underline to questionable code.

Warnings of potential problems are indicated by a green wavy underline. These are not critical and will not prevent execution of the application. A rollover **Tooltip** explains the warning.

1 In the **Code** editor, type the following variable declaration in a subroutine block, then hit **Enter**
Dim num As Integer

2 A green wavy line appears below the **num** variable name. Place the cursor over the green wavy underline to discover that the warning is merely indicating a potential problem, as the variable has not yet been assigned a value

Errors are indicated by a red wavy underline. Unlike warnings, these are critical and will prevent execution of the application. A rollover **Tooltip** explains the error.

1 In the **Code** editor, type the following variable declaration in a subroutine block, then hit **Enter**
Dim num As Integer =

2 Place the cursor over the red wavy underline to discover that the error is due to a missing value in the expression

Warnings can be ignored but errors must be corrected.

Real-time error detection in the Visual Studio IDE is a fantastic tool to help prevent errors when you are writing code. It not only indicates errors, but can even provide a list of correction options.

1 In the **Code** editor, type the following variable declaration in a subroutine block, then hit **Enter**
Dim num As Integr

2 A red wavy line appears below the **Integr** variable type. Place the cursor over the red wavy underline to discover that the error is due to an unknown type specification

3 Click the lightbulb icon, or click the **Show potential fixes** link, to see a list of error correction options

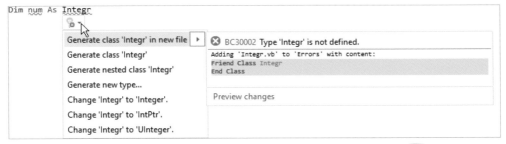

97

4 If this error is simply a spelling error for the **Integer** data type, select the option to **Change 'Integr' to 'Integer'** – see your code get instantly corrected accordingly

Other correction options enable you to create a new data type if that is what you require.

Fixing compile errors

While syntax errors like those shown on pages 96-97 can be detected by the **Code** editor in real-time, other errors that employ correct syntax cannot be detected until the code is compiled. Compile errors are typically errors of logic, and they cause the execution to halt when an "exception" occurs. For example, when incompatible data types appear in an expression, an **InvalidCastException** occurs and execution stops immediately.

1 In the **Code** editor, type the following lines into a button's Click event handler code block
```
Dim num As Double = 7.5
Dim str As String = "five"
MsgBox( num * str )
```

2 Click the **Start** button then push the button to see execution is soon halted. The line causing the exception becomes highlighted in the **Code** editor, and an **Exception Assistant** pop-up window appears

You can click on the **View Details** link in the Exception Assistant's **Actions** list for more error information.

To fix this **InvalidCastException** the code would obviously need amendment so both expression values are of the **Double** data type.

The cause of other compile errors may be less obvious without some further investigation – for example, when a loop that is reading array elements attempts to address an element index that does not exist, causing an **IndexOutOfRangeException**.

…cont'd

Execution halts immediately, so it is useful to examine the counter value to identify the precise iteration causing the compile error.

1 In the **Code** editor, type the following variable declaration and loop into a button's Click event handler code block
```
Dim i, nums(10) As Integer
For i = 1 To 20
        nums(i) = i
Next
```

2 Click the **Start** button then push the button to see execution is soon halted. The code causing the exception becomes highlighted in the **Code** editor, and an **Exception Assistant** pop-up window appears with a list of possible solutions

3 Place the cursor over the counter variable to see a pop-up appear, showing its current value

It's now clear that execution halted when the loop attempted to address **nums(11)** – beyond the bounds of last element **nums(10)**. To fix this **IndexOutOfRangeException** the code would need amendment to end the loop after 10 iterations.

Another common compile error is the **FileNotFoundException** that occurs when a file is missing or its path name is incorrect.

Debugging code

It is sometimes useful to closely examine the progression of a program by watching its execution line by line to locate any bugs. Progress is controlled by clicking the ⊞ **Step Into** button on the **Debug** Taskbar to move through the program one line at a time. When you begin debugging you can open a **Watch** window to monitor the value of particular variables as execution proceeds.

1 Double-click on a Form to open the **Code** editor in its **Load** event-handler, then add the following code

```
Dim i As Integer
Dim pass As Integer = 0
Dim base As Integer = 2
For i = 1 To 2
        pass = pass + 1
        base = Square( base )
Next
```

2 Now, add this arithmetic function into the declarations section of the code with these lines

```
Function Square(ByVal num As Integer)
        num = num * num
        Return num
End Function
```

3 In the **Code** editor, click in the gray margin against the **Load** event-handler – to set a debug starting "breakpoint"

```
● 23 |  Private Sub Form1_Load(sender As Object, e As EventArgs) Handles MyBase.Load
```

4 Click the **Step Into** button once to begin debugging

5 Click **Debug, Windows, Watch, Watch1** on the Menu Bar to launch a **Watch** window

6 Type the variable name "pass" into the **Name** column and hit **Enter**, then repeat to add the "base" variable name

Name	Value	Type
⟳ pass	0	Integer
● base	0	Integer

Don't forget

You can click the **Stop Debugging** button at any time to return to normal **Code** editor mode.

7 Click **Step Into** five times to reach the **Square** function call in the first loop iteration, and note the variable values

If you can't see the **Step Into** button, right-click on the Toolbar and select **Debug** to add the debugging buttons there.

8 Click **Step Into** eight more times to progress through each line of the **Square** function and the loop, returning to the function call on the second iteration

9 Click the ⇨ **Step Over** button once to execute the function without stepping through each line

For i = 1 To 2
    pass = pass + 1
    base = Square(base)
Next ≤2ms e

Name	Value	Type
pass	2	Integer
base	16	Integer

The ⇨ **Step Out** button is used to return to the function caller when you are stepping through lines of a called function.

10 When you have finished debugging, click the red dot you added in the margin to remove the breakpoint

Setting debug breakpoints

In all but the smallest of programs, stepping through each line is very tedious when debugging. Instead, you can quickly reach the part you wish to examine by setting a "breakpoint" to halt execution on a particular line. Setting one or more breakpoints is useful to help you understand how certain Visual Basic code constructs work – such as the nested loop construct shown here.

BreakPoint

1 Double-click on a Form to open the **Code** editor in its **Load** event-handler, and type this code
```
Dim i, j, k As Integer
Dim pass As Integer = 0
For i = 1 To 3
        For j = 1 To 3
                For k = 1 To 3
                        pass = pass + 1
                Next
        Next
Next
```

2 In the **Code** editor, click in the gray margin against each line containing the **Next** keyword to set three breakpoints – a red dot will appear in the margin and each **Next** statement is highlighted to indicate the set breakpoints

3 Click the **Start** button and see the application run to the first breakpoint it meets

Hot tip

Yellow arrows indicate the current position. Click on the red dot to cancel a breakpoint.

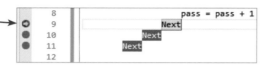

4 Click **Debug, Windows, Locals** to launch the **Locals** window and notice the current value of each variable

...cont'd

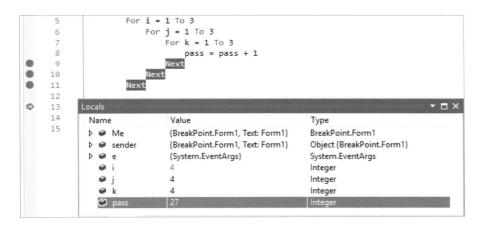

Locals			▼ □ ×
Name	Value	Type	
▷ ● Me	{BreakPoint.Form1, Text: Form1}	BreakPoint.Form1	
▷ ● sender	{BreakPoint.Form1, Text: Form1}	Object {BreakPoint.Form1}	
▷ ● e	{System.EventArgs}	System.EventArgs	
● i	1	Integer	
● j	1	Integer	
● k	1	Integer	
⊘ pass	1	Integer	

5 Watch the variable values change as you repeatedly click the **Start** (**Continue**) button to move to each **Next** breakpoint until you reach the third outer **Next** statement, then click **Step Into** to reach the end of the subroutine

The **Locals** window shows all variables in current scope as the program proceeds.

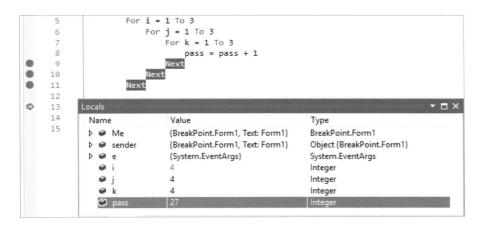

```
5        For i = 1 To 3
6            For j = 1 To 3
7                For k = 1 To 3
8                    pass = pass + 1
9            Next
10       Next
11   Next
12
13
14
15
```

Locals			▼ □ ×
Name	Value	Type	
▷ ● Me	{BreakPoint.Form1, Text: Form1}	BreakPoint.Form1	
▷ ● sender	{BreakPoint.Form1, Text: Form1}	Object {BreakPoint.Form1}	
▷ ● e	{System.EventArgs}	System.EventArgs	
● i	4	Integer	
● j	4	Integer	
● k	4	Integer	
⊘ pass	27	Integer	

At the end of the subroutine each counter variable has been incremented beyond the upper limit set in the **For** statements, to exit each loop, and there has been a total of 27 iterations (3x3x3).

6 Click **Stop Debugging** to finish, then click the **Start** button to once more run to the first breakpoint

7 Click **Debug**, **Windows**, **Immediate** to launch the **Immediate** window

8 In the **Immediate** window, type **i = 3** and hit **Enter**, then use the **Step Into** button to step through each line of the final complete outer loop iteration

Any code you type into the **Immediate** window is dynamically applied to the application being debugged, but does not change its code. Try typing **MsgBox("Hi")** into the **Immediate** window, then hit the **Enter** key.

103

VB

RunTime

Detecting runtime errors

While the **Code** editor provides real-time detection of syntax errors, and the compiler provides detection of logic errors, it is the responsibility of the programmer to anticipate user actions that may cause runtime errors when the application is in use. Consideration of all the different ways a user could employ your application is important to predict potential runtime errors.

1 In a new project add **Label**, **TextBox**, and **Button** controls to a Form, so it looks like this:

2 Name the yellow **Label** "LblResult"

3 Double-click on the "Add" button to open the **Code** editor in its **Click** event-handler, then type the code below to create a simple adding machine
```
Dim num1 As Integer = Val( TextBox1.Text )
Dim num2 As Integer = Val( TextBox2.Text )
LblResult.Text = num1 + num2
```

4 Click the **Start** button, then enter numeric values into each text field and click the "Add" button to see the application perform as expected

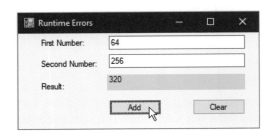

Adding floating point values with this application will produce a result rounded to the nearest integer.

...cont'd

5 Now, try adding large numbers like those shown here – an error will occur and the system will halt the program, complaining of an overflow

While the programmer may not have intended the application to be used to add such large numbers, it is possible the user may wish to do so – and this possibility should have been considered in order to predict this type of runtime error. The overflow has, in fact, occurred because the **Integer** data type can only store numeric values up to around two billion. This problem can be fixed by changing the variables to use a **Long** data type instead.

The precise value range of the **Integer** data type is -2,147,483,648 through 2,147,483,647.

6 Quit the application, then edit the "Add" button's **Click** event-handler to read like this:

```
Dim num1 As Long = Val( TextBox1.Text )
Dim num2 As Long = Val( TextBox2.Text )
LblResult.Text = num1 + num2
```

7 Save the amended project, then run the application and try to add the two long numbers again

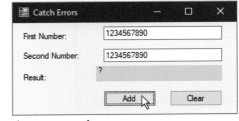

CatchErrors

Catching runtime errors

When you are able to predict potential runtime errors by considering all eventualities, you can provide code to handle exceptions that may arise with a **Try Catch** code block. Your program can supply information to the user about the error, should you wish to do so, then proceed normally. This technique could be used to provide code to handle the exception that arose in the previous example on page 105, instead of the fix suggested.

1 Repeat steps 1, 2, and 3 on page 104 to recreate the simple adding machine application, then click the **Start** button to run the application in **Debug** mode

2 Enter two long numbers, then click the "Add" button to attempt the addition – the compiler reports that an **OverflowException** has occurred

Hot tip

You can use the right-click context menu to quickly switch between the **Code** editor and the Form **Designer**.

3 Click the **Stop Debugging** button so you can edit the code

4 Right-click in the "Add" button's **Click** event-handler code block, then choose **Snippet, Insert Snippet, Code Patterns, Error Handling (Exceptions)** from the context menu

...cont'd

5 Double-click **Try...Catch...End Try Statement** to paste a **Try Catch** code block into the **Code** editor

```
Try

Catch ex As ArgumentException

End Try
```

6 In place of **ArgumentException** in the pasted code block, type "OverflowException" – to catch that sort of error

7 Cut and paste the original lines of code to put them between the **Try** and **Catch** lines

8 Add this code between the **Catch** and **End Try** lines **MsgBox("only numbers up to 2 Billion are allowed")**

```
Try

    Dim num1 As Integer = Val(TextBox1.Text)
    Dim num2 As Integer = Val(TextBox2.Text)
    LblResult.Text = num1 + num2

Catch ex As OverflowException

    MsgBox("only numbers up to 2 Billion are allowed")

End Try
```

9 Click the **Start** button, then enter long numbers as before, and click the "Add" button to see the exception handled

CatchErrors

only numbers up to 2 Billion are allowed

OK

10 Click **OK** to close the **MsgBox,** then change the numbers to be within the range allowed, and click the "Add" button to proceed normally

Insert Snippet contains lots of useful pieces of code to paste into the **Code** editor – take some time to explore its contents.

Try adding code to handle the exceptions on page 98 and 99 instead of the suggested fixes.

107

The **Help Viewer** is no longer installed by default when you install Visual Studio unless you select it from the Individual Components list.

The **Help Viewer** allows you to download **Help** libraries for offline use, check for available updates, and seek help from installed **Help** libraries.

Getting help

The Visual Studio **Help** system provides an extensive source of reference for many programming languages. You can choose to install a Help Library on your computer for the Visual Basic programming language so you can easily refer to it at any time, but the Help Viewer must first be installed in Visual Studio:

1 Click **Visual Studio Installer** on your apps menu, then click the **Modify** button on the Installer dialog

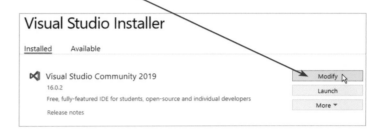

2 Select the **Individual Components** tab, check the **Help Viewer** option, then click the **Modify** button to install

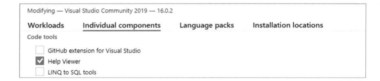

3 On the Visual Studio Menu Bar, click **Help**, **Add and Remove Help Content** to open the **Help Viewer**

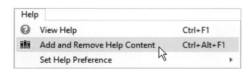

4 On the **Manage Content** tab, expand **Recommended Documentation**, then choose the **Add** link in the **Action** column for the **Visual Basic** library

5 When your selection is added to the **Pending changes** list, click the **Update** button to download that library

...cont'd

6 On the Menu Bar, click **Help**, **Set Help Preference**, **Launch in Help Viewer** to use installed library

You can **Set Help Preference** to **Launch in Browser** if you want to search online help without installing libraries, but local help is often more convenient.

109

7 Next, click **Help**, **View Help** to launch **Help Viewer**

8 Now, select the **Index** tab in the left-hand pane

9 Type the item for help, such as "data types", in the **Help Viewer** Search box, then hit **Enter** to see the results

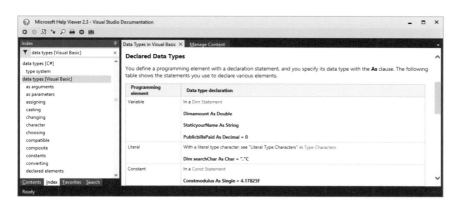

Summary

- The **Code** editor constantly monitors your code to provide real-time error detection.

- Warnings are not critical and are indicated by a green wavy underline – whereas errors are critical and are indicated by a red wavy underline.

- A lightbulb box at the end of a red wavy underline indicates that a list of possible corrections is available.

- Typically, real-time errors are errors of syntax, and compile errors are errors of logic.

- When a compile error occurs in **Debug Mode**, execution stops and the **Exception Assistant** offers a list of possible fixes.

- In **Debug Mode** you can discover the current value of any variable simply by placing the cursor over the variable name.

- The **Step Into** button lets you walk through a program one line at a time.

- The **Step Over** button lets you bypass the lines of a called function, and the **Step Out** button lets you return to the line where that function is called.

- Variable values can be monitored as a program proceeds using the **Watch** window or the **Locals** window.

- Breakpoints halt the execution of a program to allow examination of the part of the program where they are set.

- In **Debug Mode**, code can be dynamically applied using the **Immediate** window.

- Runtime errors occur when the user action has not been anticipated by the programmer.

- Use a **Try Catch** block to handle anticipated exceptions.

- The **Help** library system provides extensive reference sources for both offline and online assistance.

7 Extending the interface

This chapter demonstrates how applications can incorporate dialogs, menus, multiple forms, and Windows Media Player.

Color, Font & Image dialogs

The Visual Studio IDE makes it simple to add the ability to call upon the standard Windows selection dialogs, so the user can choose options within your applications – for example, for selection of colors, fonts, and images.

ColorFontImageDialogs

1 Create a new **Windows Forms App** project and add a **PictureBox**, **TextBox**, and three **Button** controls to the Form – arranged as shown below

Hot tip

Set the TextBox's **Multiline** property to **True** so you can make it taller than a regular single line.

2 Next, name the **Button** controls **BtnColor**, **BtnFont**, and **BtnImage**

3 From the **Dialogs** section of the **Toolbox** add a **ColorDialog**, **FontDialog**, and **OpenFileDialog** component to the Form – see them appear in the **Component Tray** at the bottom of the Form Designer

4 Double-click on the **BtnColor Button** and add this code to its **Click** event-handler
```
If ColorDialog1.ShowDialog = DialogResult.OK Then
        Me.BackColor = ColorDialog1.Color
End If
```

5 Double-click on the **BtnFont Button** and add this code to its **Click** event-handler
```
If FontDialog1.ShowDialog = DialogResult.OK Then
        TextBox1.Font = FontDialog1.Font
End If
```

6 Double-click on the **BtnImage Button** and add this code to its **Click** event-handler

```
If OpenFileDialog1.ShowDialog = DialogResult.OK Then
  Try
        PictureBox1.Image = _
        New Bitmap(OpenFileDialog1.FileName)
  Catch ex As ArgumentException
        MsgBox("Not an image")
  End Try
End If
```

Beware

The **OpenFileDialog** allows the user to select any file. The **Try Catch** statement handles the **ArgumentException** that is thrown if the user chooses a file type that is not an image.

7 Click on the **Start** button to run the application, then click the **BtnColor Button** to launch the familiar Windows **Color** selection dialog

8 Choose a color, then click the **OK** button to apply it to the Form's background

113

9 Type some text in the **TextBox**, then click the **BtnFont Button** and choose a Font for that text

10 Click the **BtnImage Button**, then browse to select an image to assign to the **PictureBox** control

Hot tip

The chosen font here is Mistral (36pt), and the chosen image is a logo in PNG format on a transparent background.

Open, Save & Print dialogs

Applications created with Visual Basic can call upon the standard Windows selection dialogs to allow the user to open, save and print files.

OpenSavePrintDialogs

1 Create a new **Windows Forms App** and add a **RichTextBox** and three **Button** controls to the Form – name the **Button** controls **BtnOpen, BtnSave**, and **BtnPrint**

2 From the **Dialogs** section of the Toolbox add an **OpenFileDialog** and **SaveFileDialog** component, then add a **PrintDialog** component from the **Printing** section of the Toolbox – see them appear in the **Component Tray** at the bottom of the Form Designer

3 Double-click on the **BtnOpen Button** and add this code to its **Click** event-handler

```
With OpenFileDialog1
        .Title = "Open File"
        .Filter = "Rich Text Files | *.rtf"
        .FileName = ""
        .CheckFileExists = True
End With

If OpenFileDialog1.ShowDialog = DialogResult.OK Then
  RichTextBox1.LoadFile(OpenFileDialog1.FileName, _
        RichTextBoxStreamType.RichText)
End If
```

Always define filter options to determine which file types the **OpenFileDialog** can recognize.

4 Double-click on the **BtnPrint Button** and add this code to its **Click** event-handler

```
If PrintDialog1.ShowDialog = DialogResult.OK Then

' Insert code here to process and print.

End If
```

...cont'd

Double-click on the **SaveBtn** Button and add this code to its **Click** event-handler

```
With SaveFileDialog1
        .Title = "Save File"
        .Filter = "Rich Text Files | *.rtf"
        .DefaultExt = ".rtf"
        .OverWritePrompt = True
End With

If SaveFileDialog1.ShowDialog = DialogResult.OK Then
    RichTextBox1.SaveFile(SaveFileDialog1.FileName, _
        RichTextBoxStreamType.RichText)
End If
```

6 Click on the **Start** button to run the app, then use the **BtnOpen Button** to launch the familiar Windows **Open File** dialog

Choose a Rich Text File (**.rtf**) on your computer, then click **Open** to load it in the **RichTextBox** control

8 Click the **BtnSave Button** to launch the familiar **Save File** dialog, and save the loaded file with a different name

9 Click on the **BtnPrint Button** to launch the familiar Windows **Print** dialog to select **Printer preferences**

The **Print** dialog does not automatically know how to print the document – you need to provide code to enable printing. See page 151 for an example of how to print plain text documents.

Creating application menus

Drop-down menus, toolbars, and status bars, like those found in most Windows applications, can easily be added to your own Visual Basic applications from the Toolbox.

Jotter

1 Find the **Menus & Toolbars** section of the **Toolbox**, then double-click the **MenuStrip** item to add it to the Form

2 Click the **MenuStrip** control's arrow button on its **Smart Tag**, then select the **Insert Standard Items** option

3 When the familiar headings and items have been added to the **MenuStrip**, right-click on any item and use the context menu to edit that item. Also, type new custom items into the **Type Here** boxes as required

You can create your own custom menus using the **Type Here** boxes instead of **Insert Standard Items**.

4 In the **Toolbox**, double-click on the **ToolStrip** item to add it to the Form, then click its **Smart Tag** button and once more select **Insert Standard Items**

5 When the familiar icon buttons have been added to the **ToolStrip**, right-click on any item and use the context menu to edit that item. Also, add further custom items from the drop-down list as required

6 In the **Toolbox**, double-click on the **StatusStrip** item to add it to the Form

7 Select the **StatusLabel** item from the StatusStrip drop-down list, then set its **Text** property to "Ready"

Use **StatusBar** messages to provide feedback to the user.

8 Add a **RichTextBox** control to the center of the Form, click its **Smart Tag** button and select the option to **Dock in parent container**, then ensure that its **ScrollBars** property is set to **Both**

Jotter (cont'd)

Be careful not to double-click on the menu item's name unless you want to edit the default keyboard shortcut – click at the side of the name to open the **Code** editor.

Making menus work

The menu items and toolbar buttons created on pages 116-117 will not perform their desired actions until you add some code to make them work. For actions that feature both in a menu and on a toolbar button, it is best to create a subroutine that can be called from the menu item's **Click** event-handler and the button's **Click** event-handler – to avoid duplication.

1 In Form Designer, click **File**, **New** to select the **New** menu item

2 Double-click on the **New** menu item to open the **Code** editor in its event-handler, and add this call
NewFile()

3 Immediately below the **End Sub** line of the **New** menu item's event-handler, add this custom subroutine
Private Sub NewFile()
  RichTextBox1.Text = ""
  ToolStripStatusLabel1.Text = "Ready"
End Sub

4 Return to the Form **Designer**, then double-click on the **New** toolbar button to open the **Code** editor in that event-handler and add a call to the custom subroutine
NewFile()

5 Add an **OpenFileDialog** and **SaveFileDialog** component from the **Dialogs** section of the **Toolbox**

6 In the **Click** event-handlers of both the **Open** menu item and the **Open** toolbar button, add this code
OpenFile()

7 Immediately below the **End Sub** line of the **Open** menu item's event-handler, add this custom subroutine

```
Private Sub OpenFile()
  OpenFileDialog1.Filter = "Text Files | *.txt"
  If OpenFileDialog1.ShowDialog = DialogResult.OK Then
    RichTextBox1.LoadFile(OpenFileDialog1.FileName, _
        RichTextBoxStreamType.PlainText)
  End If
End Sub
```

You can add functionality to the **File**, **Exit** menu item simply by adding **Application.Exit()** to its **Click** event-handler.

8 In the **Click** event-handlers of both the **Save** menu item and the **Save** toolbar button, add this code

```
SaveFile()
```

9 Immediately below the **End Sub** line of the **Save** menu item's event-handler, add this custom subroutine

```
Private Sub SaveFile()
  SaveFileDialog1.Filter = "Text Files | *.txt"
  If SaveFileDialog1.ShowDialog = DialogResult.OK Then
    RichTextBox1.SaveFile(SaveFileDialog1.FileName, _
        RichTextBoxStreamType.PlainText)
  End If
End Sub
```

10 Run the application and test the functionality of the **New**, **Open**, and **Save** file menu items and toolbar buttons

Keyboard shortcuts are already configured – try **Ctrl** + **N**, **Ctrl** + **S**, and **Ctrl** + **O** to test them.

Adding more forms

Most Windows applications have more than one Form – even the simplest application usually has an **About** dialog, and perhaps a **Splash Screen**, to provide version information to the user. These can easily be added to your applications in Visual Basic.

Jotter (cont'd)

1 Click **Project, Add New Item** on the Menu Bar, to launch the **Add New Item** dialog, then select the **About Box** icon and click the **Add** button

2 Select **Project, Jotter Properties** on the Menu Bar, to open the **Project Designer** window, then choose **Application** and click the **Assembly Information...** button

3 Modify the **Copyright**, **Description**, and **Company** fields, then click **OK**

4 In Form **Designer**, double-click on the **About** item in the **Help** menu then add this code to its **Click** event-handler
AboutBox1.ShowDialog()

5 Click the **Start** button to run the application, then click **Help**, **About** to see the **About** dialog

Adding a Splash Screen

1 Click **Project**, **Add New Item** on the Menu Bar, to launch the **Add New Item** dialog, then select the **Splash Screen** icon and click the **Add** button

2 Click **Project**, **Jotter Properties** on the Menu Bar, to open the **Project Designer** window

3 Open the **Splash Screen** drop-down list at the bottom of the **Project Designer** window, and select **SplashScreen1**

4 Click the **Start** button to run the application and see a **Splash Screen** display for about two seconds before the main Form appears

The **Splash Screen** and **About** dialog are similar – both display information from the **Assembly Information**, but less detail is shown in the **Splash Screen** because it is only displayed briefly.

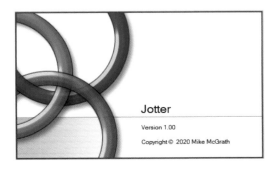

Controlling multiple forms

Applications sometimes need more than one Form to accommodate the user interface. When the user moves to the second Form, the first one can be hidden so any information it contains will remain in memory and reappear when the user returns to that Form. Similarly, the second Form can be hidden so any user input it contains is available to the program when the user returns to the first Form. Alternatively, the second Form can be closed when the user returns to the first Form, but any user input will then be lost unless it has been stored in variables.

MultipleForms

1 Add two **Button** and **Label** controls to a Form so it looks like this, and name the yellow **Label LblValue**

2 Click **Project**, **Add New Item** and add another **Windows Form** to the project

3 Add a **TextBox** and two **Button** controls to this Form, naming the Buttons **BtnClose** and **BtnHide**

Hot tip

Consider using multiple Forms when the application interface becomes cluttered with many controls.

4 In **Form Designer**, double-click on the "Hide Form 1" **Button** in **Form 1**, and add this code to its **Click** event-handler
Me.Hide()
Form2.Show()

5 Now, double-click on the "Show Hidden Value" **Button** in **Form 1** and add this code to that **Click** event-handler
LblValue.Text = Form2.TextBox1.Text

6 In **Form Designer**, double-click on the "Hide Form 2" **Button** in **Form 2** and add this code to its **Click** event-handler
```
Me.Hide()
Form1.Show()
```

7 Now, double-click on the "Close Form 2" **Button** in **Form 2** and add this code to that **Click** event-handler
```
Me.Close()
Form1.Show()
```

8 Click the **Start** button to run the application and click the "Hide Form 1" **Button** – to see that **Form 1** disappears and **Form 2** appears

9 Type something into the **TextBox**, then click on the "Hide Form 2" **Button** – **Form 2** disappears, and **Form 1** reappears

10 Click the "Show Hidden Value" **Button** in **Form 1** – the text you typed into the **TextBox** in **Form 2** gets copied into the **LblValue** **Label** in **Form 1**

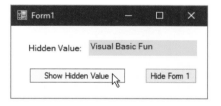

11 Click "Hide Form 1" once more, then type something else in the **TextBox** and click the "Close Form 2" **Button**

12 Click the "Show Hidden Value" **Button** in **Form 1** again – nothing is displayed in the **LblValue** **Label** as your input is now lost

Hot tip

Try creating a variable to store the value in the **TextBox** when **Form 2** gets closed, so the user input can be recalled.

PlaySound

Playing sounds

Sound files can be included within an application as a resource, in much the same way that image files can be imported as a resource, to enhance the application. These can then be played, as required, by calling upon the Windows Media Player on the local system.

1 Create a new **Windows Forms App** project and add a single **Button** control to the Form

2 Select **Project**, **PlaySound** *(ProjectName)* **Properties** on the Menu Bar, to open the **Project Designer** window

Always use the Project Designer to remove a resource – you cannot simply delete it from **Solution Explorer**.

3 In **Project Designer**, select the **Resources** side tab, then the **Audio** item from the drop-down list

4 From the **Add Resource** drop-down list, select the **Add Existing File...** item to launch the **Add existing file to resources** dialog

You can add an icon resource and assign it to the Form's **Icon** property in its **Load** event-handler.

5 Browse to the location of the sound file you wish to add, then click the **Add** button

You can typically find the Windows sound files in the folder on your computer at **C:\Windows\Media**.

6 The sound file **tada.wav** now gets added to the **Resources** folder in **Solution Explorer** and appears in the **Resources** window of **Project Designer**

7 Click the **X** tab button to close the **Project Designer**, and click **Yes** when asked if you want to save changes

8 Click **View**, **Code** on the Menu Bar to open the **Code** editor, then add this line to the declarations section
```
Friend WithEvents player _
    As New System.Media.SoundPlayer
```

A sound can be played repeatedly using the **PlayLooping()** method – the loop can be ended with the **Stop()** method.

9 In Form **Designer,** double-click on the **Button**, then add the following code to its **Click** event-handler
```
player.Stream = My.Resources.tada
player.Play()
```

10 Click the **Start** button to run the application, then click the **Button** to play the sound

125

Playing multimedia

VB

PlayMedia

A Visual Basic application can employ an **ActiveX** instance of the Windows Media Player to play all types of local media files within the application interface.

1 Create a new **Windows Forms App** project, then add a **Button** control and an **OpenFileDialog** component

2 In the **Toolbox**, right-click on the **Components** section and select **Choose Items...** from the context menu

3 When the **Choose Toolbox Items** dialog appears, click its **COM Components** tab, then check "Windows Media Player" and click **OK** – a new **Windows Media Player** item gets added to the Toolbox **Components** section

The **Common Object Model (COM)** is a standard platform that allows components to be easily shared.

4 From the **Toolbox**, add a **Windows Media Player**

component to the Form and resize it so its display and controls are fully visible – note that this component is called **AxWindowsMediaPlayer1**

...cont'd

5 In **Form Designer**, double-click on the **Button** to open the **Code** editor in its **Click** event-handler, and add the following code

```
With OpenFileDialog1
  .Title = "Media File Browser"
  .Filter = "Media Files (*.mp4;*.mp3)|*.mp4;*.mp3"
  .FileName = ""
  .CheckFileExists = True
End With

If OpenFileDialog1.ShowDialog = DialogResult.OK Then
  AxWindowsMediaPlayer1.URL = _
        OpenFileDialog1.Filename
End If
```

6 Run the application, then click the **Button** control to launch the **OpenFileDialog** and choose a valid media file – see it start playing in the application interface

Notice how multiple file formats must be separated by a semi-colon in the **Filter** statement.

Try adding a status bar to display the name of the file currently playing.

Summary

- The **Dialogs** section of the **Toolbox** contains components that can be added to an application to call upon the standard Windows dialogs to select Colors, Fonts, Images, and Files.

- **Open File** and **Save File** dialogs can be configured to filter file types so they only display files of a specified file extension.

- A **Print** dialog allows the user to select printer options, but it cannot automatically print.

- Familiar menus can easily be added to an application using the **Insert Standard Items** option of the **MenuStrip** component.

- The **ToolStrip** component provides familiar toolbar icons.

- You can add a **StatusStrip** component to provide an application status bar to display feedback to the user.

- Where both **MenuStrip** and **ToolStrip** components appear in an application it is best to create subroutines to be called when the user chooses a menu item or associated icon.

- A **MenuStrip** component automatically provides keyboard shortcuts for each of its menu items.

- The **Add New Item** option on the **Project** menu can be used to add a **Form**, **About Box** dialog, and **Splash Screen**.

- Multiple forms can be controlled using their **Show()**, **Hide()**, and **Close()** methods.

- Applications can be enhanced by including audio files in their **Resources** folder to provide sound.

- Windows **COM Components** can be added to the standard selection of components on the Visual Studio Toolbox.

- An **ActiveX** instance of Windows Media Player can be added to an interface to allow the application to play multimedia files.

8 Scripting with Visual Basic

This chapter illustrates how Visual Basic may be used outside the Visual Studio IDE to add functionality to Microsoft Office applications, and to perform useful tasks with Windows Script Host.

Introducing VBA macros

Visual Basic for Applications (VBA) is the programming language built into Microsoft Office applications. It shares the same core Visual Basic language as that in the Visual Studio IDE, but has different available objects in each application – Word has an **ActiveDocument** object, and Excel has an **ActiveSheet** object.

Where Microsoft Office is installed on a system, all Office objects are available across all versions of Visual Basic. So you can program Word from Excel, or from a stand-alone application created in the Visual Studio IDE.

VBA has a Form **Designer** and **Debugger** much like those in the Visual Studio IDE, but with a more limited set of features.

Hot tip

Most VBA keyboard shortcuts are the same as in the Visual Studio IDE.

Form Designer · Run Button · Project Window · Properties Window

Toolbox

Code Editor

You cannot create stand-alone executable applications with Visual Basic for Applications, as it has no native code compiler, but you can create a script, hidden within the document file, to execute a series of instructions upon the document. This is known as a "macro", and is typically used to automate a task you perform regularly that requires multiple commands. For example, to insert a table with a specific style and number of rows and columns.

…cont'd

1 Launch Microsoft Word, or any other Office application, then click the **Developer** tab and choose the **Visual Basic** ribbon icon to launch the **Visual Basic Editor**

Hello.docm

2 In the **Visual Basic Editor**, click **Insert**, **Module** to open the **Code** editor window

Hot tip

If the **Developer** tab is not visible, click **File**, **Options**, **Customize Ribbon**, and check the "Developer" box in the **Main Tabs** options.

131

3 In the **Code** editor, click the ▶ **Run** button and name the macro "Hello", then click the **Create** button

4 Now, type this line into the Visual Basic subroutine automatically created in the **Code** editor window
MsgBox("Hello from VBA!")

Hot tip

Our examples describe Office 2019. For versions of Office earlier than Office 2007, the Visual Basic Editor is launched from the **Tools**, **Macros** menu.

5 In the **Visual Basic Editor**, click the ▶ **Run** button to execute the subroutine – the Visual Basic Editor gets minimalized until you click the **OK** button in the Message Box

Creating a Word macro

Bookmarks can be inserted into a Word document to indicate the position at which a macro should insert content.

Table.docm

1 Open a new document in Word, type this book's title, then use **Insert**, **Links**, **Bookmark** to add a bookmark – and name it "mark"

2 Click **Developer**, **Visual Basic**, or press **Alt + F11**, to launch the **Visual Basic Editor**

3 In the **Visual Basic Editor**, click **Insert**, **Module** to open the **Code** editor window

4 Now, type the following code into the **Code** editor

```
Sub AddTable()
  If ActiveDocument.Bookmarks.Exists("mark") Then
    ActiveDocument.Bookmarks("mark").Select
    Set tbl = ActiveDocument.Tables.Add(Range:= _
      Selection.Range, NumRows:=3, NumColumns:=9)
    tbl.AutoFormat Format:=wdTableFormatElegant
  End If
End Sub
```

5 Click the **Run** button, to run the macro – see a formatted table appear at the bookmark position

Hot tip

You can use the **Undo** button in Word to reverse the two steps performed by VBA to Add and Format this table.

...cont'd

When you have created a macro that you wish to make available for use in other documents, the macro can be stored inside Word's master template **Normal.dotm** and added as a Word menu item.

1 Select **Developer, Macros** to open the **Macros** dialog, then click the **Organizer** button

2 Choose the **Macro Project Items** tab, select the macro module from the current document list, then click the **Copy** button to copy the macro to **Normal.dotm**

The **Run** button on the **Macros** dialog can be used to run any macro stored in **Normal.dotm** – without creating a custom menu item.

3 Close the **Organizer** and the current document, then start a new document and insert a bookmark named "mark"

4 Click **File, Options, Quick Access Toolbar**, to enter the **Customize the Quick Access Toolbar** dialog

5 In the **Choose Commands from** drop-down, choose **Macros**, then **Add** the **AddTable** module and click **OK** to add an icon to the **Quick Access Toolbar**

6 Click the newly-added **AddTable** macro icon on the **Quick Access Toolbar** to run the macro – once more adding the same formatted table at the bookmark position

Creating an Excel macro

Values can be inserted into cells of an Excel spreadsheet by a macro that uses a loop to move through a range of cells.

Year.xlsm

1 Open a worksheet in Excel, then click **Developer**, **Visual Basic**, or press **Alt + F11**, to open the **Visual Basic Editor**

2 In the **Visual Basic Editor**, click **Insert**, **Module** to open the **Code** editor window

3 Now, type the following code into the **Code** editor
```
Public Sub AddMonthNames()
  Dim i As Integer
  i = 0
  Do Until i = 12
        Set currentCell = ActiveSheet.Cells( _
          ActiveCell.Row + i , ActiveCell.Column)
        i = i + 1
        currentCell.Font.Bold = True
        currentCell.Font.Color = vbRed
        currentCell.Value = MonthName( i )
  Loop
End Sub
```

If the **Developer** tab is not visible, click **File**, **Options**, **Customize Ribbon**, and check the "Developer" box in the **Main Tabs** options.

VBA has a small range of color constants, like the **vbRed** constant seen here. Refer to VBA Help to discover a full list.

4 Select any cell in the worksheet, then click the **Run** button, to run the macro – see bold red month names appear in cells down the current column, starting at the selected cell

134

…cont'd

Excel macros can be run automatically when a Worksheet gets loaded, or manually using a **Button** control.

1 In the Visual Basic Editor's **Project** window, right-click on the **ThisWorkbook** icon and choose **View Code** from the context menu

2 From the drop-down list at the top of the **Code** editor, select the **Workbook** item, then add this code

```
Private Sub Workbook_Open()
  MsgBox("Workbook opened at " + Str(Time) )
End Sub
```

3 On the **Developer** tab, click **Insert**, **ActiveX Controls** (button) then click an empty cell to add a **Button** control

4 Double-click the **Button** control to open the **Code** editor in its **Click** event-handler, then add this statement

```
Call AddMonthNames
```

5 Save the changes and close the worksheet – reopen the worksheet to see the MessageBox appear, then click the **Button** to run the macro

135

Hot tip

Use the **Design Mode** button on the **Developer** tab when you want to edit or move controls on a worksheet.

Running advanced macros

More advanced macros can be created to control one Office application from within another. Typically, you may want to include information from an Excel spreadsheet within a Word document, using a macro to get the information automatically.

Sales.xlsx

1 Open Excel and add some data in cell **B2**. Name this cell "Total", then save the Workbook as "Sales.xlsx" in your Documents folder and close Excel

Sales.docm

2 Start a new Word document, then insert a **Bookmark** and also name it "Total" – it doesn't need to have the same name as the Excel cell, but it is convenient

3 Open the **Visual Basic Editor**, then click **Tools**, **References** to launch the **References** dialog – check the **Microsoft Excel Object Library** item, then click **OK**

Don't forget

The version number of the **Microsoft Excel Object Library** will vary according to which Office version you are using.

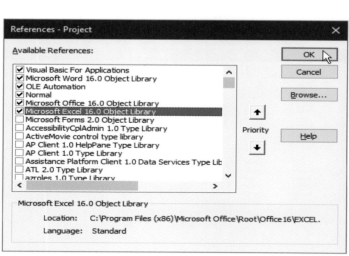

4 In the **Visual Basic Editor,** click **Insert**, **Module** to open the **Code** editor window

5 Now, type the following code into the **Code** editor, modifying the path to suit the location of your "Sales.xlsx"

```
Private Sub GetTotal()
  Set xl = CreateObject("Excel.Application")
  xl.Workbooks.Open ("C:\Users\Mike\Documents\Sales.xlsx")
  xl.Worksheets("Sheet1").Activate
  ActiveDocument.Bookmarks("Total").Select

  Dim sum As String
  sum = FormatCurrency( xl.ActiveSheet.Cells( 2, 2 ) )
  Selection.InsertAfter (sum)

  xl.Workbooks.Close
  Set xl = Nothing
End Sub
```

The Excel cell in this example is addressed as **xl.ActiveSheet.Cells(2,2)** – row 2 and column 2.

6 Click the **Run** button, to run the macro and see the value retrieved from the Excel cell get formatted into the local currency and appear in the Word document

Top Sales Award

For

Excellent Achievement

With Annual Sales of

$5,250,000.00

Remember to have the macro close the Workbook and release Excel after it has retrieved the cell value.

An introduction to VBScript

VBScript is a scripting language that, like VBA, shares the same core Visual Basic language as that found in a Visual Studio IDE. Scripts written in VBScript are interpreted by the **Windows Script Host** VBScript "engine", which processes the instructions to execute the script. The script engine can be invoked either from within the Windows GUI, or at a Windows Command Prompt.

Windows Script Host is standard in Windows 10.

Unlike the Visual Studio IDE, and VBA Code Editor in Microsoft Office apps, there is no development environment for VBScript – you simply create your scripts in any plain text editor.

Hello.vbs

1 Open a plain text editor, such as Windows Notepad, then type the following code
MsgBox "Hello from VBScript!", **vbExclamation** , "Message"

2 Name this file "Hello.vbs", and save it on your Desktop

3 Double-click on the file icon to invoke the **Windows Script Host** VBScript engine from the Windows GUI to execute the script – see the Message Box appear

4 Launch a **Command Prompt** window, then use the CD command to navigate to your Desktop directory

5 Type the command "Hello.vbs", and hit **Enter** to invoke the **Windows Script Host** VBScript engine from the Command Prompt – see the Message Box appear again

Notice that VBScript does not have any parentheses in the statement that creates the message box dialog.

Enforcing declarations

It is good practice to begin every VBScript with a statement of **Option Explicit**. This is a standard "compiler directive" that must appear at the start of a script, and requires all variables to be explicitly declared with the **Dim** keyword before they can be used. Without this directive, the script can implicitly create variables simply by assigning a value to a variable name of your choice. Although this might seem harmless, it can create unexpected errors that can be difficult to debug. Adding **Option Explicit** at the start of the script provides error-checking to prevent these errors. Its significance can best be understood by a simple example:

1 Create a script that assigns a text string to an implicit variable to be displayed in a message box dialog
bookTitle = "Visual Basic in easy steps"
MsgBox bookTile, vbInformation, "Message"

Explicit.vbs

2 Run the script to see that the string fails to appear, as the variable name is misspelled on the second line – the compiler thinks this is just another implicit variable so gives no warning

3 Edit this script by adding these lines, at the very start of the script, to enforce and comply with variable declaration
Option Explicit
Dim bookTitle

4 Run the script once more to see the error clearly identified, as the misspelled variable name has not been declared

Hot tip

You should always begin each and every VBScript with the **Option Explicit** compiler directive.

5 Correct the spelling error then run the script to see it now performs as expected

Validating input

VBScript is a topic in itself, but to get a flavor of how it can be used, the rest of this chapter is devoted to three scripts that handle user input, text files, and Windows registry data, respectively.

As with Visual Basic, VBScript can request user data with an input dialog box. The input data is assigned to a variable as a text string that can be examined for validation against requirements. For example, to allow only letters and space characters:

GetName.vbs

1 Start a VBScript with the standard compiler directive, then declare a variable to store input, and a variable to store an expression against which to validate the input
Option Explicit
Dim name, regX

2 Add a function block that assigns input to the **name** variable and has a placeholder for test statements
Private Function GetName()

name = InputBox("What's Your Name?", "Question")

' If-Else statements to be inserted here.

End Function

3 At the placeholder, insert a test to exit the script if the user pushes the "Cancel" button on the input dialog
If VarType(name) = vbEmpty Then
Exit Function

Hot tip

The **VarType()** function returns an integer indicating the data type of the variable. Where the variable is uninitialized (such as when the user presses the Cancel button), it returns zero – equivalent to the constant **vbEmpty**.

4 Next, insert a test to inform the user if they input nothing, then re-open the input dialog so they can try again
Elseif name = "" Then
MsgBox "You didn't input anything", _
                            vbInformation, "Error"
Call GetName

5 Now, insert a test to inform the user of invalid input, then re-open the input dialog so they can try again
Elseif Invalid() Then
MsgBox "Only A-Z and Spaces Allowed!", _
                            vbCritical, "Error"
Call GetName

6 Finally, insert a statement to display valid accepted input

```
Else
MsgBox "Welcome " & name & "!" , _
                vbExclamation, "Message"
End If
```

7 Add a second function that implements character validation by testing against a Regular Expression

```
Private Function Invalid()
  Set regX = New RegExp
  regX.Pattern = "[^A-Z a-z]"
  Invalid = regX.Test( Name )
End Function
```

The **RegExp** object has a **Pattern** property, that specifies valid characters, and a **Test()** method to compare a specified value against its pattern.

8 At the end of the script, add a statement to call the first function, requesting user input

```
Call GetName
```

9 Run the script and attempt to validate various input

Learn more about Regular Expressions online at **regular-expressions.info**

Merging text files

Just as the previous example made use of a scripting object called "RegExp", which provided special properties and methods to handle Regular Expressions, there is a scripting object called "Scripting.FileSystemObject" that provides special properties and methods to handle a computer's file system.

Once you have created an instance of the **FileSystemObject**, you can open folders and files to read and write within the file system. For example, you can use its methods and properties to copy text from multiple existing files into a single new file:

FileMerge.vbs

1. Create a folder named "Textfiles" on your Desktop, then place several plain text files within that folder

Beware

Note that the **GetFolder()** method here specifies the name and path to the folder. If you name your folder differently, or put it elsewhere, you will need to modify those details in the **Set folder** statement.

2. Start a VBScript with the standard compiler directive, then declare five variables for text file manipulation
Option Explicit
Dim fso, folder, textOut, file, textIn

3. Add a statement to create a **FileSystemObject** instance
Set fso = CreateObject("Scripting.FileSystemObject")

4. Next, add a statement to get a list of the names of all files within the "Textfiles" folder
Set folder = fso.GetFolder(".\Textfiles").Files

5. Now, add a statement to create a new text file – into which you can copy text from each file within the folder
Set textOut = fso.CreateTextFile("Merged.txt")

6 Add a loop that opens then closes each file within the folder, and has a placeholder for read/write statements
For Each file In folder

    Set textIn = fso.OpenTextFile(file, 1)

    ' Read/write statements to be inserted here.

    textIn.Close

Next

7 At the placeholder, insert statements to write each file's name, text content, and a blank line separator
textOut.WriteLine "File: " & file.Name
textOut.WriteLine textIn.ReadAll
textOut.WriteLine vbCr

8 At the end of the script, after the loop, add a statement to close the new file after all content has been written into it
textOut.Close

9 Save the script on your Desktop, alongside the "Textfiles" folder, then run the script and open the new file it creates

The numeric value specified to the **OpenTextFile()** method indicates the input/output mode. A value of 1 is ForReading mode, a value of 8 is ForAppending mode.

This script must be in the same directory as the Textfiles folder, or you will need to modify the path in the **Set folder** statement.

Getting registry data

The Windows operating system has a scripting object called "WScript.Shell" that provides special properties and methods to handle environment variables, shortcuts, and Registry components. For example, you can use its methods and properties to get the Windows version name, product ID, and product key. The key is stored in encrypted format, but it can be decrypted by VBScript:

WinInfo.vbs

 Start a VBScript with the standard compiler directive, then declare five variables for registry manipulation
Option Explicit

Dim wss, dir, sys, pid, bin

 Add a statement to create a **Shell** object instance
Set wss = CreateObject("WScript.Shell")

 Next, initialize the remaining four variables with a registry location path and values read from that location
dir = _
"HKLM\SOFTWARE\Microsoft\Windows NT\CurrentVersion\"
sys = "Version: " & _
      wss.RegRead(dir & "ProductName") & vbCr
pid = "ID: " & wss.RegRead(dir & "ProductID") & vbCr
bin = wss.RegRead(dir & "DigitalProductId")

 Add a statement to display the Windows information
MsgBox sys & pid & "Key: " & Decrypt(bin), _
        vbInformation, "WinInfo"

 Add a function block that receives the encrypted binary key read from the registry – that is to be decrypted
Private Function Decrypt(bin)

' Statements to be inserted here.

End Function

6 Within the function block, begin by declaring 10 variables, then initialize three of them, like this
Dim win, map, i, j, cut, seq, fin, top, add, serial

win = (bin(66) \ 6) And 1
bin(66) = (bin(66) And &HF7) Or ((win And 2) * 4)
map = "BCDFGHJKMPQRTVWXY2346789"

Beware

Changing values in the Windows Registry can render your PC useless. This script merely reads existing values without making changes to the Registry.

7 Add these nested loops to interpret the encrypted key

```
i = 24
Do
        cut = 0
        j = 14
        Do
                cut = cut * 256
                cut = bin( j + 52 ) + cut
                bin( j + 52 ) = ( cut \ 24 )
                cut = cut Mod 24
                j = j -1
        Loop Until j < 0
        i = i - 1
        seq = Mid( map, cut + 1, 1 ) & seq
        fin = cut
Loop Until i < 0
```

This script example is not intended to be instructional – it merely demonstrates the power of VBScript.

8 Now, add these statements to make substitutions

```
top = Mid( seq, 2, fin )
add = "N"
seq = Replace( seq, top, top & add, 2, 1, 0 )
If fin = 0 Then seq = add & seq
```

9 Add these final statements to format and return the decrypted key to the calling statement for display

```
serial = ""
For i = 1 To 25
        serial = serial + Mid( seq, i, 1 )
        If ( i Mod 5 = 0 ) And ( i < 25 ) Then
                serial = serial + "-"
        End If
Next
Decrypt = serial
```

From Windows 8 onwards, the product key is no longer visible on a case sticker but is encrypted in the Registry – this script helps you retrieve your key.

10 Run the script to see the Windows version and product information displayed

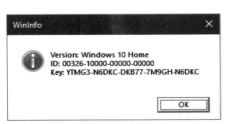

Summary

- Visual Basic for Applications (VBA) is built into all Microsoft Office applications, but each application has unique objects.

- The VBA environment is similar to that of the Visual Studio IDE, but it can't produce stand-alone executable applications.

- A **macro** can insert content into a Word document at the position indicated by an inserted bookmark.

- Saving macros in the **Normal.dotm** master template makes them available for use in other Word documents.

- Loops can be used in a VBA macro to read or write a range of cells within an Excel spreadsheet.

- Advanced macros allow one Office application to be controlled from within another one.

- There is no development environment for VBScript – scripts are created in any plain text editor such as Windows Notepad.

- The script engine that interprets VBScript instructions can be invoked from the Windows GUI or at the Command Prompt.

- Every VBScript should begin with an **Option Explicit** statement to enforce declaration of variables before their use.

- The **VarType()** function that tests variable data types will return a **vbEmpty** zero value when the tested variable is uninitialized.

- A **RegExp** object has a **Pattern** property and a **Test()** method for Regular Expression comparison – such as input validation.

- A **Scripting.FileSystemObject** object has properties and methods to read and write text files on your system.

- The **OpenTextFile()** method must specify whether the file is being opened in ForReading mode or in ForAppending mode.

- A **WScript.Shell** object has properties and a methods to handle environment variables, shortcuts, and Registry components.

9 Harnessing data

This chapter shows how Visual Basic applications can import data from a variety of external sources.

Reading text files

The **My.Computer.FileSystem** object has methods that make it easy for Visual Basic applications to work with local files. Text can be imported using its **ReadAllText()** and exported using its **WriteAllText()** method to append text to an existing file, or create a new file. Files can be removed with the **DeleteFile()** method, or their existence confirmed with the **FileExists()** method.

ReadWriteText

1 Create a new **Windows Forms App** then add two **TextBox** controls and three **Button** controls to the Form

2 Set the **Multiline** property of the bottom **TextBox** to **True**, then name the buttons **BtnWrite, BtnRead, BtnDelete**

3 Select **View, Code** to open the **Code** editor, then create a path variable in the declarations section, modifying the path to that of the Documents folder on your system
Dim myFile As String = "C:\Users\mike_\Documents\log.txt"

Remember to include the third **True** parameter to append text to a file.

4 Double-click on **BtnWrite** to open the **Code** editor, and add the following code to its **Click** event-handler
```
My.Computer.FileSystem.WriteAllText( _
      myFile, TextBox1.Text & vbCrLf, True)
TextBox1.Text = ""
```

5 Return to the Form **Designer,** then double-click **BtnRead** and add this code to its **Click** event-handler
```
Try
  TextBox2.Text = _
  My.Computer.FileSystem.ReadAllText( myFile )
Catch ex As Exception
  TextBox2.Text = "Unable to read from " & myFile
End Try
```

6 Return to the Form **Designer**, then double-click
BtnDelete and add this code to its **Click** event-handler
```
TextBox1.Text = ""
TextBox2.Text = ""
If My.Computer.FileSystem.FileExists( myFile ) Then
  My.Computer.FileSystem.DeleteFile( myFile )
End If
```

Ensure that the
application has
permission to write to
the log file location.

7 Click the **Start** button to run the application, then enter
some text into the top **TextBox**

log.txt

8 Click **BtnWrite** to have your text written into a new file
and see the top **TextBox** become cleared

9 Click **BtnRead** to have the file contents read and see your
text appear in the bottom **TextBox**

Remove the log file,
then click **BtnRead** to
attempt to read from the
missing file – the **Catch**
statement will appear.

10 Repeat Steps 7 and 8 to append more lines of text, then
click **BtnDelete** to remove the file and text content

Streaming lines of text

The Visual Basic **System.IO** class can be used to import data and files into an application as a "stream". A stream is more flexible than a file, as it can be searched and manipulated. A stream is first created as a new **System.IO.FileStream** object that specifies the file to work with and the operation to perform as its parameters. A new **System.IO.StreamReader** object can then be created to read from an opened file in a variety of ways – its **ReadToEnd()** method will read the entire file. It is important to then release the **StreamReader** and **FileStream** using their **Dispose()** method.

StreamText

1. Add to a Form an **OpenFileDialog**, a **TextBox**, and two **Button** controls named **BtnOpen** and **BtnPrint**

2. Double-click on the **OpenBtn Button** to open the **Code** editor, then add this code to the declarations section
   Dim txt As String

3. Now, add the following code to the **BtnOpen Button** control's **Click** event-handler
   ```
   If OpenFileDialog1.ShowDialog = DialogResult.OK Then
     Dim stream As New System.IO.FileStream _
     (OpenFileDialog1.FileName, System.IO.FileMode.Open)
     Dim reader As New System.IO.StreamReader(stream)
   txt = reader.ReadToEnd
   reader.Dispose()
   stream.Dispose()
   TextBox1.Text = txt
   End If
   ```

4. Run the application, then click the **BtnOpen Button** and browse to select a text file for display in the **TextBox**

ideal.txt

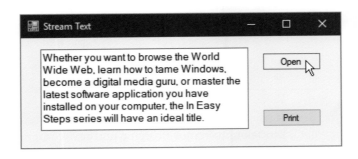

Adding Print ability

1 Add both a **PrintDialog** and **PrintDocument** component from the **Printing** section of the **Toolbox**

2 Double-click on the **BtnPrint Button** and add the following code to its **Click** event-handler
```
PrintDialog1.AllowSomePages = True
PrintDialog1.ShowHelp = True
If PrintDialog1.ShowDialog = DialogResult.OK Then
  If txt <> "" Then
    PrintDocument1.Print()
  End If
End If
```

The **PrintDialog** component lets your application launch the Windows **Print** dialog – but you need to add a **PrintDocument** component to actually print anything.

This subroutine configures the **Print** dialog, then if the **txt** variable is not empty, calls the **Print()** method of the **PrintDocument1** component. This is not enough to print by itself – it merely fires a **PrintPage** event whose event-handler must be coded to make the application print out the text.

3 Double-click on the **PrintDocument1** icon in the Form Designer's **Component Tray** to open the **Code** editor in its **PrintPage** event-handler, and type this code
```
e.Graphics.DrawString(txt, Me.Font, Brushes.Black, _
e.MarginBounds, StringFormat.GenericTypographic)
```

In this code the letter "e" is specified in the event-handler's parameters to represent a **PrintPageEventArgs** object that uses the **Graphics.DrawString()** method to print the text.

4 Click the **Start** button to run the application and use the **BtnOpen Button** to choose a text file, then click the **BtnPrint Button** to send it to your printer

Further code would need to be added to the **PrintPage** event-handler to allow the printer to handle multiple pages.

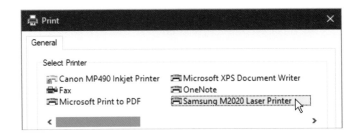

Reading Excel spreadsheets

Data contained within an Excel spreadsheet can be imported into an application where the value of each cell can be conveniently stored in a two-dimensional array, representing rows and columns. This allows each individual cell to be addressed using the same row and column number that it has in the spreadsheet – for instance, **cell(2,3)** could address the third cell on the second row.

Data.xlsx

1 Create an Excel Workbook called "Data.xlsx" with the data values below, and save it in your **Documents** folder

ReadCells

2 Create a new **Windows Forms App**, then add three **ListBox** and **Label** controls, and a **Button** to the Form

Refer to page 136 for an illustration of the **References** dialog – compare the similarities in this example with the VBA example listed there.

3 Click **Project, Add Reference** to launch the **Add Reference** dialog, then choose the **Microsoft Excel Object Library** item on the **COM** tab, and click **OK**

4 Select **View, Code** to open the **Code** editor, then create a path variable to the spreadsheet in the declarations section
Dim mySS As String = "C:\Users\Mike\Documents\Data.xlsx"

5 Double-click on the **Button** control to open the **Code** editor, and type this code into its **Click** event-handler

```
Dim row, col, finalRow, finalCol As Integer
Dim xl = CreateObject("Excel.Application")
xl.Workbooks.Open( mySS )
xl.Worksheets("Sheet1").Activate()
finalRow = xl.ActiveSheet.UsedRange.Rows.Count
finalCol = xl.ActiveSheet.UsedRange.Columns.Count
Dim vals(finalRow, finalCol) As String
```

This opens the Worksheet, counts the number of used rows and columns, then create a two-dimensional array of the same size.

6 Add this loop to assign the cell values to the array elements and to display them in the **ListBox** controls

```
For row = 1 To finalRow
  For col = 1 To finalCol
    vals(row, col) = Str(xl.ActiveSheet.Cells(row, col).Value)
    ListBox1.Items.Add(row)
    ListBox2.Items.Add(col)
    ListBox3.Items.Add( vals(row, col) )
  Next col
Next row
```

7 Finally, add these two lines to release the resources, then run the application and click the **Button**

```
xl.Workbooks.Close()
xl = Nothing
```

Many examples in this book benefit by enclosure in a **Try Catch** statement but they are not listed in order to save space – add one to this example to catch the exception that would be thrown if the Worksheet could not be read.

153

Read Cells		
Row	**Column**	**Value**
1	1	1001
1	2	1002
1	3	1003
2	1	2001
2	2	2002
2	3	2003
3	1	3001
3	2	3002
3	3	3003

Get Data

See page 63 for more on multi-dimensional arrays.

Reading XML files

The Visual Basic **System.Xml** object can be used to easily import data into an application from an XML document. A container for the data is first created as a **System.Xml.XmlDocument** object, then the data is loaded into it using its **Load()** method to copy data from the XML document file.

A **System.Xml.XmlNodeList** can then create an **Item()** array of all the elements in the XML document. Individual elements can be addressed by stating their name as the parameter to the **SelectSingleNode()** method of the **Item()** array, and the value contained within that element retrieved by its **InnerText** property.

1 Open any plain text editor, such as **Notepad**, and create an XML document with elements like those below – name it **Books.xml** and save it in the **Documents** folder

Books.xml

Don't forget

You can download the XML document shown here, along with all the other files used in this book, from www.ineasysteps. com/resource-centre/ downloads/

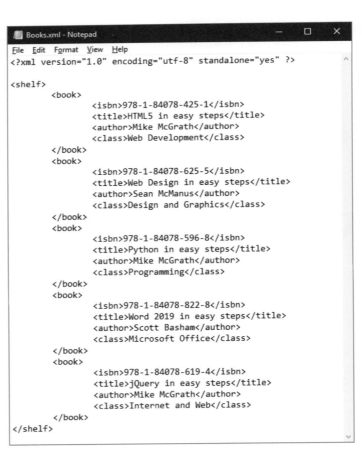

```xml
<?xml version="1.0" encoding="utf-8" standalone="yes" ?>

<shelf>
        <book>
                <isbn>978-1-84078-425-1</isbn>
                <title>HTML5 in easy steps</title>
                <author>Mike McGrath</author>
                <class>Web Development</class>
        </book>
        <book>
                <isbn>978-1-84078-625-5</isbn>
                <title>Web Design in easy steps</title>
                <author>Sean McManus</author>
                <class>Design and Graphics</class>
        </book>
        <book>
                <isbn>978-1-84078-596-8</isbn>
                <title>Python in easy steps</title>
                <author>Mike McGrath</author>
                <class>Programming</class>
        </book>
        <book>
                <isbn>978-1-84078-822-8</isbn>
                <title>Word 2019 in easy steps</title>
                <author>Scott Basham</author>
                <class>Microsoft Office</class>
        </book>
        <book>
                <isbn>978-1-84078-619-4</isbn>
                <title>jQuery in easy steps</title>
                <author>Mike McGrath</author>
                <class>Internet and Web</class>
        </book>
</shelf>
```

2 Create a new **Windows Forms App** and add a **ListBox** and a **Button** to the Form

ReadXmlData

3 Double-click on the **Button** to open the **Code** editor, and type this code into its **Click** event-handler to create an **XmlDocument** object from the XML file

```
Dim doc As New System.Xml.XmlDocument
doc.Load( "C:\Users\Mike\Documents\Books.xml" )
```

4 Add the following code to create an **XmlNodeList** from the **<book>** elements and their nested elements

```
Dim nodes As System.Xml.XmlNodeList
nodes = doc.SelectNodes( "shelf/book" )
```

5 Now, add a loop to display the text contained in each **<title>** and **<author>** element, then run the application

```
Dim counter = 0
Do Until counter = nodes.Count
  ListBox1.Items.Add(nodes.Item(counter) _
  .SelectSingleNode("title").InnerText & " by " _
  & nodes.Item(counter) _
  .SelectSingleNode("author").InnerText & vbCrLf)
  counter += 1
Loop
```

Notice how the **Count** property of the **XmlNodeList** is used to set the limit of the loop.

Creating an XML dataset

Visual Basic provides specialized components for working with data in table format, such as that contained in XML elements or database tables. These components can be found in the **Toolbox** under the **Data** heading.

The **DataSet** component can be added to an application to create a table in the system memory that can be loaded with data from any suitable source. Most often it is convenient to display the table data in the interface using a **DataGridView** component. This allows the data stored in the memory to be dynamically manipulated within the application then written back to a file.

XmlDataSet

1   Create a new **Windows Forms App**, and add a **DataGridView** component and two **Button** controls to the Form – name the buttons **BtnRead** and **BtnWrite**

Here, the document file **Books.xml** must be located in the **Documents** directory – adjust the path to suit your system.

2   Double-click on the **DataSet** item in the **Toolbox**, then choose the **Untyped DataSet** option in the **Add DataSet** dialog and click **OK** – see the **DataSet** icon appear on the **Component Tray** in the Form Designer

3   Double-click the **BtnRead Button** to open the **Code** editor, then type this code into its **Click** event-handler to create a **DataSet** from the XML document on page 154
DataSet1.ReadXml("C:\Users\Mike\Documents\Books.xml" **)**

4   Add this code to load those elements nested under the **<book>** element from the **DataSet** into the **DataGridView** control
DataGridView1.DataSource = DataSet1
DataGridView1.DataMember = "book"

5 Return to the **Form Designer**, then double-click the **BtnWrite Button** and add this code to its event-handler
DataSet1.WriteXml("C:\Users\Mike\Documents\Books.xml")

6 Click the **Start** button to run the application, then click the **BtnRead Button** to load the **DataSet** data into the **DataGridView** control

XML Data Set				
isbn	title	author	class	
▶ 978-1-84078-425-1	HTML5 in easy steps	Mike McGrath	Web Development	Get Data
978-1-84078-625-5	Web Design in easy steps	Sean McManus	Design and Graphics	
978-1-84078-596-8	Python in easy steps	Mike McGrath	Programming	
978-1-84078-822-8	Word 2019 in easy steps	Scott Basham	Microsoft Office	Write XML
978-1-84078-619-4	jQuery in easy steps	Mike McGrath	Internet and Web	

You can set a DataGridView's **AutoSizeColumnsMode** property to **AllCells** to automatically show all text content in each cell.

The **DataGridView** control displays the element name as the heading for each column and the element content on each row of that column. Initially, the first cell on the first row is in focus, but you can click on any other cell to move the focus. When you double-click the cell in focus, it changes into edit mode where you can update its content.

7 Add another row of data to the last row of the table, then click the **BtnWrite** control to save the amended data

XML Data Set				
isbn	title	author	class	
978-1-84078-425-1	HTML5 in easy steps	Mike McGrath	Web Development	Get Data
978-1-84078-625-5	Web Design in easy steps	Sean McManus	Design and Graphics	
978-1-84078-596-8	Python in easy steps	Mike McGrath	Programming	
978-1-84078-822-8	Word 2019 in easy steps	Scott Basham	Microsoft Office	
978-1-84078-619-4	jQuery in easy steps	Mike McGrath	Internet and Web	Write XML
▶ 978-1-84078-824-2	Excel VBA in easy steps	Mike McGrath	Microsoft Office	

ScrollBars will, by default, automatically appear when the cell content overflows the DataGridView control. Setting its **ScrollBars** property to **None** can hide content from view.

8 Restart the application, then click the **ReadBtn Button** to once more load the XML data into the **DataGridView** control – see that the row you added has been preserved

Reading RSS feeds

Live XML data can be imported from outside the local system into a Visual Basic application using a **Really Simple Syndication (RSS)** feed. This delivers the XML data as a stream that can be stored within a **System.Xml.XmlDocument** object, like that used to store data from an XML file on page 155.

OpenWeatherMap

A free RSS feed is available from "OpenWeatherMap" to provide current weather data. To request the feed you need to supply certain parameters stating your unique API key ("APPID"), preferred data mode (XML), preferred temperature units ("metric" for Celsius), and required location (e.g. US ZIP code).

1 First, browse to **openweathermap.org** and **Sign Up** to get your own free unique APPID (API key)

2 Enter this URL into the address field of your browser to request a feed – inserting your own APPID
**api.openweathermap.org/data/2.5/weather?
appid=APPID&mode=xml&units=metric&zip=10021**

3 The feed response will be an XML document containing elements and attributes similar to the one shown below

```
<current>
  <city id="420027057" name="New York">
    <coord lon="-74" lat="40.79" />
    <country>US</country>
    <sun rise="10:06:52" set="23:41:50" />
  </city>
  <temperature value="14.2" unit="celsius" />
  <humidity value="93" unit="%" />
  <pressure value="1017" unit="hPa" />
  <wind>
    <speed value="1.78" name="Light breeze" />
    <gusts />
    <direction value="348.823" />
  </wind>
  <clouds value="90" value="overcast clouds" />
  <visibility value="16093" />
  <precipitation mode="no" />
  <weather number="83" value="overcast clouds" />
  <lastupdate value="2022-04-23T05:30:00" />
</current>
```

VB

ReadRssFeed

Hot tip

In the XML document the elements are colored purple, attributes are colored red, and values are colored blue. Each of these can be represented in an XmlNodeList object for use in Visual Basic.

4 Now, create a new **Windows Forms App,** then add a **GroupBox, Label, Button,** and **TextBox** control to the Form

5 Name the **TextBox** as TxtZip, and set its **Text** property to "10021" – a New York City zip code – then arrange the controls, like this:

You can find the **GroupBox** control in the **Containers** section of the **Toolbox**.

6 To create a request query to OpenWeatherMap for the city above, double-click on the **Button** and type the following code into its **Click** event-handler – each on a single line!
```
Dim rssUrl = "http://api.openweathermap.org/data/2.5/
weather?appid=APPID&mode=xml&units=metric&zip="
+ TxtZip.Text

Dim rssRequest As System.Net.WebRequest =
System.Net.WebRequest.Create(rssUrl)
```

You must your insert your own APPID here.

7 Save the response data into a **Stream** object by adding these two statements
```
Dim rssResponse As System.Net.WebResponse = _
        rssRequest.GetResponse()

Dim rssStream As System.IO.Stream = _
        rssReponse.GetResponseStream
```

8 Type the code below to load the saved data stream into an **XmlDocument** object
```
Dim rssDoc As New System.Xml.XmlDocument
rssDoc.Load(rssStream)
```

Addressing XML attributes

ReadRssFeed(cont'd)

9 Create an **XmlNodeList** of all elements below the root **<current>** element of the **XmlDocument** object
```
Dim nodes As System.Xml.XmlNodeList
nodes = rssDoc.SelectNodes("current")
```

10 Now, add this code to display the value of the **name** attribute that is within the **<city>** element of the **XmlDocument** object
```
GroupBox1.Text = _
nodes.Item(0).SelectSingleNode("city/@name").InnerText
```

11 Run the application and click the **OK** button to test the RSS request – after a short delay see the **GroupBox Text** property change to the city named in the response

This example relies upon the format of an external XML document – if the format gets changed it may need amendment to run correctly.

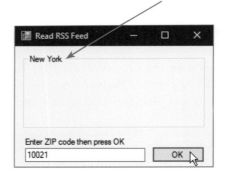

12 Now you know that the request is receiving a response, add three **TextBox** and three **Label** controls to the Form

13 Name the **TextBox** controls **TxtClimate**, **TxtTemperature**, and **TxtHumidity**, and set the **Text** property of each **Label**

14 Add this code to display the current weather condition
```
TxtClimate.Text = nodes.Item(0). _
SelectSingleNode("weather/@value").InnerText
```

15 Add this code to display the current temperature
```
TxtTemperature.Text = nodes.Item(0). _
SelectSingleNode("temperature/@value").InnerText + "C"
```

Notice how the /@ characters are used here to denote the name of an attribute.

16 Add this code to display the current humidity
```
TxtHumidity.Text = nodes.Item(0). _
SelectSingleNode("humidity/@value").InnerText+ "%"
```

17 Run the app, then click the **OK** button to retrieve the current weather information for any given ZIP code

18 Surround the entire code in the **Click** event-handler to catch an exception if the RSS feed is not accessible, then disconnect from the internet and run the app again
```
Try
  ' All error-handler code goes here.
Catch err As System.Net.WebException
  MsgBox(err.Message)
End Try
```

You can see more about **Try Catch** statements back on page 106.

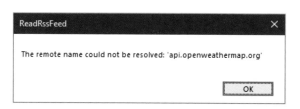

Summary

- The **My.Computer.FileSystem** object can be used to read and write files on your computer.

- A **System.IO.Stream** object can store text that has been read from a local file or external source, such as a web response.

- It is important to dispose of **System.IO.Stream** and **System.IO.StreamReader** objects after they have been used.

- The **Print()** method of a **PrintDocument** component does not actually send data to your printer – it only fires a **PrintPage** event whose event-handler must be coded in order to print.

- Data imported from an Excel spreadsheet can best be stored in a two-dimensional array representing rows and columns.

- The **System.Xml.XmlDocument** object is used to store a representation of an XML document.

- A **System.Xml.XmlNodeList** object creates an **Item()** array of elements selected from a **System.Xml.XmlDocument**.

- The **InnerText** property of a node contains the actual content of that element.

- A **DataSet** component creates a table in system memory that can be loaded with data from any suitable source.

- It is often convenient to display **DataSet** table data in a **DataGridView** component – where it can be modified then written from system memory back to the original source.

- An application can request an RSS feed using a **System.Net.WebRequest** object.

- A **System.Net.WebResponse** object handles the response received after requesting an RSS feed.

10 Employing databases

This chapter introduces databases, and demonstrates how to add powerful database functionality to a Visual Basic application with SQL Server.

An introduction to databases

Microsoft SQL Server
is the relational database
management system
developed by Microsoft.

Databases are simply convenient storage containers that store data in a structured manner. Every database is composed of one or more tables that structure the data into organized rows and columns. This makes it easy to reference and manipulate the data. Each database table column has a label to identify the data stored within the table cells in that column. Each row is an entry called a "record", which places data in each cell along that row, like this:

MemberID	Forename	Surname
1	John	Smith
2	Ann	Jones
3	Mike	McGrath

The rows of a database table are not automatically arranged in any particular order, so they can be sorted alphabetically, numerically, or by any other criteria. It is important, therefore, to have some means to identify each record in the table. The example above allocates a "MemberID" for this purpose, and this unique identifier is known as the **Primary Key** for that table.

Storing data in a single table is useful, but relational databases with multiple tables introduce more possibilities by allowing the stored data to be combined in a variety of ways. For example, the table below could be added to the database containing the table shown above.

Spaces are not allowed
in label names – so you
should use "MemberID"
instead of "Member ID".

BookID	Title	MemberID
1	The Dreamers	2
2	Becoming	3
3	How We Win	1

The table lists book titles sorted numerically by "BookID" and describes a relationship linking each member to a borrowed book:
John (**MemberID #1**) has "How We Win" (**BookID #3**)
Ann (**MemberID #2**) has "The Dreamers" (**BookID #1**)
Mike (**MemberID #3**) has "Becoming" (**BookID #2**)

In this table, the **BookID** column has the **Primary Key** values identifying title records in this table, and the **MemberID** column in this table contains **Foreign Key** values that reference member name records in the first table.

SQL Server

The SQL Server DataBase Management System (DBMS) that can be bundled with Visual Studio adheres to the relational model like other Relational DataBase Management System (RDBMS) software such as Oracle or IBM DB2. This means that it observes "normalization" rules that you need to be aware of when designing a database.

Data normalization

Normalization rules insist that data is organized efficiently, and without duplication or redundancy, in order to reduce the potential for anomalies when performing data operations. They require each table to have a **Primary Key** column, and permissible data types must be defined for all other columns. This determines whether cells in the column may contain text or numbers, within a specified range, and whether cells may be left empty or not. In considering the design of a database, normalization sensibly requires data to appear only once – so any repeated data should be moved into its own table then referenced where required. For example, where customer name and address details are repeated in two tables, they should be moved to their own table that can then be referenced from each of the two original tables. This makes it easier to update the customer details without the possibility of creating an anomaly by updating just one set of data.

Data integrity

Another important aspect of RDBMS software concerns the preservation of data integrity by prohibiting "orphaned" records. This means that records that are referenced in another table cannot be deleted unless the reference is first deleted. Otherwise the reference would become orphaned, as it could not find the data in its "parent" table. For example, where a table of customer order details contains a reference to a record in a table of products, the RDBMS software will not allow the product record to be deleted, as doing so would render the customer order reference useless.

A **Foreign Key** always references a **Primary Key** in another table – name them both alike for easy recognition.

The SQL Server Data Tools may not have been installed along with Visual Basic – run the installer, click **Modify**, **Individual components**, then check **SQL Server Data Tools** and install them.

Designing a database

The process of database design is typically one of refinement to recognize the rules of normalization. Start out with a single table design for all data fields, then move those that are repeating into their own table.

Consider the design for a database to store data about an imaginary range of motorcycles comprising "Sport", "Cruiser", and "Touring" models that are selectively available in "Standard", "Deluxe", and "Classic" versions, and where each model/version has a unique price. A single **Bikes** table of the entire range, plus a column for individual notes, might look like this:

BikeID	Model	Version	Price	Note
1	Sport	Standard	5000	
2	Sport	Deluxe	5500	
3	Cruiser	Standard	6000	
4	Cruiser	Deluxe	6500	
5	Cruiser	Classic	7000	
6	Touring	Standard	8000	
7	Touring	Classic	9000	

The **BikeID** column provides a unique identifier for each row, and can be set as the **Primary Key** for the table. The **Price** column contains unique values, and all cells in the **Note** column are initially empty. **Model** and **Version** columns both contain repeating data in contravention of the normalization rules, so they should each be moved into separate tables like those below:

A **Primary Key** uniquely identifies a row within a database table – so a Primary Key value should never be changed.

ModelID	Model
1	Sport
2	Cruiser
3	Touring

VersionID	Version
1	Standard
2	Deluxe
3	Classic

The **ModelID** and **VersionID** columns provide a unique identifier for each row, and can be set as the **Primary Key** (PK) for their table – and they can also be used as a **Foreign Key** (FK) in the refined **Bikes** table below:

BikeID (PK)	ModelID (FK)	VersionID (FK)	Price	Note
1	1	1	5000	
2	1	2	5500	
3	2	1	6000	
4	2	2	6500	
5	2	3	7000	
6	3	1	8000	
7	3	3	9000	

In considering permissible data types for each column, in line with normalization rules, the **BikeID**, **ModelID**, **VersionID**, and **Price** columns should each allow only integer values. The **Model** and **Version** columns should only allow up to 10 characters, and the **Note** column should allow up to, say, 50 various characters. All except the **Note** column are required to contain data – in database terms they should be "Not Null". The database diagram below illustrates these data constraints and the table relationships:

In setting data constraints, consider future eventualities – might a new **Model** or **Version** perhaps have a name longer than 10 characters?

This design is used on the ensuing pages to create an SQL Server database and a Visual Basic application that can communicate with it to dynamically retrieve and manipulate data.

Creating a database

SQL Server is well integrated with Visual Studio so you can easily create a new database from within the IDE.

BikesApp

1 Create a new **Windows Forms App** project and name it "BikesApp"

2 Click **View, Solution Explorer** – to open the Solution Explorer window

3 In the **Solution Explorer** window, right-click on the **BikesApp** icon then choose **Add, New Item** from the menu – to launch the **Add New Item** dialog

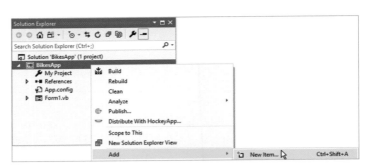

4 In the **Add New Item** dialog, select the **Service-based Database** icon, type "BikesDB.mdf" in the name field, then click the **Add** button

Hot tip

If the **Server-based Database** fails to be added you may need to install SQL Server Data Tools. Run the Visual Studio Installer, click **Modify**, **Individual components** then select **SQL Server Data Tools**, and install them.

...cont'd

Connecting to a database

1 In **Solution Explorer**, right-click the **BikesDB.mdf** icon that has been added, then choose **Open** from the context menu – to open the **Server Explorer** window

You can open the **Server Explorer** window by choosing **View**, **Server Explorer** on the Menu Bar, or double-click on the **BikesDB.mdf** icon in **Solution Explorer**.

2 Examine the **BikesDB.mdf** icon in **Server Explorer**, and you should see it has an "electric-plug" below it to indicate you are connected to that database

3 Right-click the **BikesDB.mdf** icon in **Server Explorer**, then choose **Close Connection** on the context menu – see the icon change to indicate no connection

4 Next, right-click the **BikesDB.mdf** icon in **Server Explorer**, then choose **Refresh** to reconnect to the database – see that the icon has the "electric-plug" below it once more, indicating you are connected again

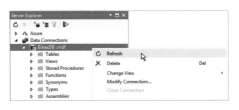

5 Now, right-click the **BikesDB.mdf** icon again and choose **Modify Connection**, to launch the **Modify Connection** dialog, and click its **Test Connection** button

6 See the **Test connection succeeded** confirmation dialog appear, then click the **OK** button on both dialogs to close them

This chapter builds a complete database application. To recreate this application it is important you carefully follow each step, in precisely the same sequence, in order to avoid errors later.

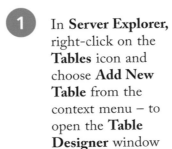

Adding database tables

Having created the **BikesDB** database on page 169, you can begin to add the **Bikes**, **Models**, and **Versions** tables from the database design on page 167, by creating the tables and setting the **Primary Key** column for each table.

1 In **Server Explorer,** right-click on the **Tables** icon and choose **Add New Table** from the context menu – to open the **Table Designer** window

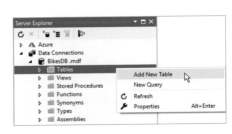

2 In **Table Designer**, type "BikeID" in the field below the **Name** heading – this will be the table's **Primary Key**

3 Click below the **Data Type** heading, then choose the **int** item from the drop-down options – to allow only integer data values for the **BikeID**

4 Ensure that the **Allow Nulls** checkbox is not checked – so empty cells will not be allowed in this column

5 Right-click on the **BikeID** box and choose **Properties** – to open that column's properties dialog

6 In **Properties**, expand the **Identity Specification** item, then set its **Is Identity** property to **True** – to have the column automatically number its rows

When working with table **Design** you can close the **Form Designer** window to clean up the IDE.

The table should have a key icon in the box before the name, denoting this as the primary key. If it doesn't, right-click in that box and choose **Set Primary Key**.

7 By default, a new table is named "Table". Edit this name in the **T-SQL** (Transact SQL) code area at the bottom of the **Table Designer** to rename this table "Bikes"

You can double-click any table icon in **Server Explorer** to re-open that table in **Table Designer**.

8 Click the **Update** link at the top-left of the table **Design** window, to open the **Preview Database Updates** dialog, then click the **Update Database** button to create the table

9 Precisely repeat each of these steps to create the **Models** table, with a "ModelID" **Primary Key**, and to create the **Versions** table with a "VersionID" **Primary Key**

See the table names also change in the **Table Designer** when you apply your updates.

10 In **Server Explorer**, right-click the **Tables** icon and choose **Refresh** to see your updates applied here – icons appear for all the new tables you have created

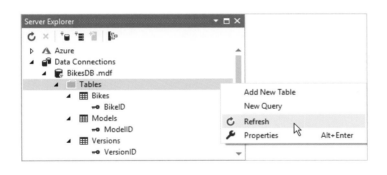

171

Defining table columns

Having created the **Bikes**, **Models**, and **Versions** tables on pages 170-171, you can begin to define other columns for each table, setting their **Name**, **Data Type**, and **Allow Nulls**.

1 In **Server Explorer**, right-click on the **Bikes** table icon in the **Tables** folder, then choose **Open Table Definition** from the context menu to open it in **Table Designer**

2 Click the next line under the **Name** heading, below the box containing the **BikeID** name, then type "ModelID" to name that column, set the data type to **int**, and uncheck the **Allow Nulls** checkbox

3 Repeat Step 2 to define the **VersionID** and **Price** columns

4 Add a column named **Note**, set the data type to **varchar(50)**, and do check the **Allow Nulls** checkbox – so the completed table definition looks like this:

The **Note** column is the only column in any of these tables that is permitted to contain an empty cell.

5 In **Server Explorer**, double-click on the **Models** table icon, or choose **Open Table Definition** from the right-click context menu, to open it in **Table Designer**

6 Click the next line under the **Name** heading, below the box containing the **ModelID** name, then type "Model" to name that column, set the data type to **char(10)**, and uncheck the **Allow Nulls** checkbox

7 In **Server Explorer**, double-click on the **Versions** table icon to open it in **Table Designer**

8 Click the next line under the **Name** heading, below the box containing the **VersionID** name, then type "Version" to name that column, set the data type to **char(10)**, and uncheck the **Allow Nulls** checkbox

9 Click the **Update** button to apply all the table changes, then **Refresh** the database contents in **Server Explorer**

10 Expand the tables in **Server Explorer** – to see all the defined columns you have created

When a table is open in **Table Designer** you can click **View**, **Properties Window** to discover properties of that table.

173

Making table relationships

Having defined all the table columns on pages 172-173, you can now establish the relationship between the tables to recognize the links for the **Bikes** table's **ModelID** column to the **Models** table, and its **VersionID** column to the **Versions** table.

1 In **Server Explorer,** right-click on the **Bikes** table icon, then choose **Open Table Definition** from the menu

2 Right-click on the **Foreign Keys** item in the right-hand pane, then choose **Add New Foreign Key** from the menu

Hot tip

You can use the **Switch to T-SQL Pane** option to open the code area full screen, then tab between **Table Designer** and the **T-SQL** code window.

3 Click anywhere on the pane and see a line get added to the **T-SQL** code area at the bottom of **Table Designer** – this must be edited to describe the table relationship

```
CONSTRAINT [FK_Bikes_ToTable] FOREIGN KEY ([Column]) REFERENCES [ToTable]([ToTableColumn])
```

4 Rename the **CONSTRAINT** from "FK_Bikes_ToTable" to **FK_Bikes_To_Models**

Don't forget

The **Constraint** name simply describes the names of the two tables associated by the **Foreign Key**.

5 Rename the **FOREIGN KEY** from "Column" to **ModelID**

6 Rename the **REFERENCES** from "ToTable (ToTableColumn)" to **Models (ModelID)**

```
CONSTRAINT [FK_Bikes_To_Models] FOREIGN KEY ([ModelID]) REFERENCES [Models]([ModelID])
```

7 Click the **Update** button at the top-left of the **Table Designer** window, then click the **Update Database** button to create the **Foreign Key** associating the **Bikes** and **Models** tables

8 Right-click on the **Foreign Keys** item in the right-hand pane, then again choose **Add New Foreign Key** from the menu

9 Click anywhere on the pane and once more see a line get added to the **T-SQL** code area in **Table Designer**

```
CONSTRAINT [FK_Bikes_ToTable] FOREIGN KEY ([Column]) REFERENCES [ToTable]([ToTableColumn])
```

10 Rename the **CONSTRAINT** from "FK_Bikes_ToTable" to **FK_Bikes_To_Versions**

11 Rename the **FOREIGN KEY** from "Column" to **VersionID**

12 Rename the **REFERENCES** from "ToTable (ToTableColumn)" to **Versions (VersionID)**

```
CONSTRAINT [FK_Bikes_To_Versions] FOREIGN KEY ([VersionID]) REFERENCES [Versions]([VersionID])
```

13 Click the **Update** link at the top-left of the **Table Designer** window, then click the **Update Database** button to create the **Foreign Key** associating the **Bikes** and **Versions** tables

14 See that the new **Foreign Key** items now appear listed in the right-hand pane in **Table Designer**

The **Foreign Keys** are associating the **ModelID** and **VersionID** columns in the **Bikes** table with the **Primary Keys** in the **Models** and **Versions** tables.

Entering table data

Having established the tables relationship on page 175, you can now begin to enter actual data records into each table.

1 In **Server Explorer**, expand the **Tables** tree then right-click on the **Models** table icon and choose **Show Table Data** from the menu, to open that table in the **Table Data** window

2 Click under the **Model** heading and type "Sport", then press **Tab** twice to move to the **Model** column on the next row – see numbering automatically appear in the **ModelID** column as its **Is Identity** property is set **True**

3 Type "Cruiser" on the second row and "Touring" on the third row so the table looks like this – then click the **X** button to close this window

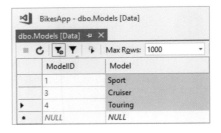

4 Open the **Versions** table in the **Table Data** window, then under the **Version** column enter "Standard" on the first row, "Deluxe" on the second, and "Classic" on the third row – then click the **X** button to close this window

You can move from row to row and from column to column using the arrow keys on your keyboard.

...cont'd

5 Open the **Bikes** table in the **Table Data** window, then enter the data from the colored table on page 167 – use the **Tab** key to move through the cells to enter **ModelID**, **VersionID**, and **Price** data so the table looks like this:

Hot tip

If you encounter an error message when entering table data it is probably because the table constraints do not allow that entry – check the table definition to correct the problem.

BikeID	ModelID	VersionID	Price	Note
1	1	1	5000	NULL
2	1	2	5500	NULL
3	2	1	6000	NULL
4	2	2	6500	NULL
5	2	3	7000	NULL
6	3	1	8000	NULL
7	3	3	9000	NULL

6 To test that the table constraints are working correctly, click the **ModelID** cell on row 1 and change its value to text, then press the **Tab** key – an error dialog should appear complaining that this entry is invalid

Microsoft Visual Studio

Invalid value for cell (row 1, column 2).

The changed value in this cell was not recognized as valid.
.Net Framework Data Type: Int32
Error Message: Input string was not in a correct format.

Type a value appropriate for the data type or press ESC to cancel the change.

OK

Don't forget

You can test the **Foreign Key** constraints are working by trying to delete any row from the **Models** or **Versions** table – you should see a dialog appear saying you cannot do so.

7 Press the **Esc** key to revert back to the original cell value, then click the **X** button to close the **Table Data** window

Creating a database dataset

Having created a database with related tables and data entries, over the last few pages, you can now proceed to develop the **BikesApp** program to incorporate the data as a **Dataset**.

1 Click **View**, **Other Windows**, **Data Sources** on the Menu Bar – to open the **Data Sources** window

2 In the **Data Sources** window, click **Add New Data Source** – to open the **Data Source Configuration Wizard**

3 Select the **Database** icon and click **Next** to proceed, then select the **Dataset** icon and click **Next** once more

4 Select **BikesDB.mdf** as the chosen connection in the drop-down list, then click **Next** to continue

Hot tip

You can click the **+** button to view the Connection string.

5 Check the **Yes, save the connection as** checkbox, to save the "BikesDB_ ConnectionString", then click **Next**

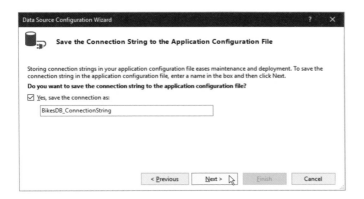

6 Check the **Tables** checkbox to include all the database tables in the dataset, then click the **Finish** button

7 In **Solution Explorer**, see that the **Dataset** has been created as a new XML Schema Document (**.xsd**) and the application configuration is stored in an XML document named **App.config**

A **Dataset** is an in-memory representation of the tables in the database that can be manipulated before writing data back to the tables.

Adding form data controls

Having created a database **Dataset** on page 179, you are now ready to add controls to the Form to display the data.

1 In **Solution Explorer,** double-click on the **Form1.vb** icon – to open the empty form in **Form Designer**

2 Click **View, Other Windows, Data Sources** to open the **Data Sources** window

Beware

The arrow button will not appear in the **Data Sources** window unless **Form Designer** is open.

3 Select the **Bikes** icon, then click on the drop-down arrow button that appears and choose the **Details** option

4 Expand the **Bikes** tree, select any item, then click the arrow button that appears, to see a list of possible controls. Choose **ComboBox** for **ModelID** and **VersionID** columns, and choose **TextBox** for all other columns

Don't forget

The icon against each item in the **Bikes** list indicates the type of control it will appear in.

5 Get ready to experience one of the most stunning features in Visual Studio! Click on the **Bikes** icon in the **Data Sources** window, then drag it across the IDE and drop it onto the empty form in **Form Designer** – see lots of controls get automatically added to the Form, and see these five items get added to the **Component Tray**

Two **ComboBox** and three **Textbox** controls are added to the Form, as specified in the **Data Sources** drop-down list, plus a navigation **ToolStrip** and

Label controls matching the column headings.

The items added to the **Component Tray** are non-visual components to manage the data flow:

● **TableAdapterManager** is the top-level component that coordinates the update operations of **TableAdapters**.

● **TableAdapter** is the data access object that has **Fill()** and **GetData()** methods to actually supply data to the controls.

● **DataSet** contains data tables of the in-memory representation of the database tables.

● **BindingSource** is an intermediate manager between the dataset and Form controls.

● **BindingNavigator** supports the navigation **ToolStrip** to move through the records, and allows data to be added or deleted.

6 Press the **Start** button to run the application and try out the navigation controls – see the **Bikes** table data appear in the **TextBox** and **ComboBox** controls

You can view a graphic representation of the DataSet – right-click on the **BikesDBDataSet** icon in the Data Sources window and choose **Edit DataSet with Designer**.

Binding meaningful data

Having added data controls to the Form on pages 180-181, you can now display the data contained in the **Bikes** table, but the **ModelID** and **VersionID** fields are still displaying the ID number – not the associated value from the linked table. To correct this so the application displays meaningful data, it is necessary to bind the linked tables to those controls.

Hot tip

If the **Form Designer** window is not visible, double-click the Form icon in **Solution Explorer** to open it.

Don't forget

All the data binding settings are made automatically when you bind the linked tables to the **ComboBox** controls.

1 Click on the **Models** table icon in the **Data Sources** window, then drag it to **Form Designer** and drop it onto the **ModelID ComboBox** control – see **ModelsBindingSource** and **ModelsTableAdapter** items get added to the **Component Tray**

2 Click on the **Versions** table icon in the **Data Sources** window, then drag it to **Form Designer** and drop it onto the **VersionID ComboBox** control – see **VersionsBindingSource** and **VersionsTableAdapter** items get added to the **Component Tray**

3 In Form Designer, click the arrow button on each **ComboBox** control to reveal their new data binding settings on the **Smart Tag**

The **ModelID ComboBox** control is now bound to **ModelsBindingSource** so will now display the **Model** value, rather than its ID number.

Similarly, the **VersionID ComboBox** is now bound to the **VersionsBindingSource** so will now display the **Version** value, rather than its ID number.

4 Edit the **Label** control alongside each **ComboBox** to remove the "ID" text – reflecting the new value these controls will display

5 As the **BikeID** is not really meaningful to the user, set its **Visible** property to **False** in the **Properties** window, then delete its **Label** control

6 Run the application and see meaningful values appear

7 To test the ability to save data into the database, enter text in the **Note** field and click the **Save Data** button

8 Use the arrow buttons to move to a different item, then return to see that your text has been preserved

Hot tip

Saved data is not preserved permanently when running in Visual Studio's debug mode, but you can run **BikesApp.exe** in the project's **bin/Debug** folder to see saved data is preserved permanently.

Building custom SQL queries

Having added the ability to display meaningful data on pages 182-183, you can now exploit the true power of databases by building custom SQL queries to extract only specific data.

1 Select the **BikesTableAdapter** icon in the **Component Tray**, then choose **Add Query...** from its **Smart Tag** options to launch the **Search Criteria Builder** dialog

The **Search Criteria Builder** dialog displays an SQL query named "FillBy" that is executed by the form's **Load** event-handler to populate the navigation **ToolStrip** and Form fields. This query selects all columns and rows of the **Bikes** table. It can be recreated as a custom SQL query that can be executed to perform the same service whenever the user requires all data to be selected.

2 Change the **New query name** field to "GetAll", then click **OK** – see another **ToolStrip** get added to the Form containing a button labeled **GetAll**

3 Select the new **ToolStrip**, then in the **Properties** window, set its **AutoSize** to **False** and change its **MaximumSize** and **Size** properties to resemble a single button **100, 30**

To create custom SQL queries that select specific data, you can simply edit the default query by appending a qualification clause.

4 Click the **BikesTableAdapter** component icon and choose **Add Query** to open **Search Criteria Builder** again

5 Change the **New query name** field to "GetClassics", then append this code to the **Query Text** statement
WHERE VersionID = 3

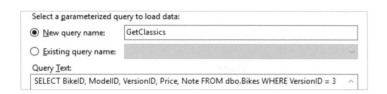

Select a parameterized query to load data:
- ⦿ New query name: GetClassics
- ○ Existing query name:

Query Text:
SELECT BikeID, ModelID, VersionID, Price, Note FROM dbo.Bikes WHERE VersionID = 3

6 Click **OK** to create a **ToolStrip** for this query, and resize it as before to resemble a single button

7 Reopen **Search Criteria Builder** and create a new query named "GetCruisers", appending this to the **Query Text** WHERE ModelID = 2

8 Resize the new **ToolStrip** as before, then run the application and click the **GetClassics** button to select data on all "Classic" versions only

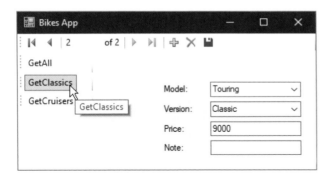

9 Click **GetAll** to select all data once more, then click **GetCruisers** to select data on all "Cruiser" models only

The navigation **ToolStrip** shows the number of records selected by that query – in this case, two "Classic" versions and three "Cruiser" models.

Summary

- Databases store data in structured rows and columns, making it easy to reference and manipulate data.

- Each row in a database table is called a record and must have a **Primary Key** to uniquely identify that record.

- A table in a relational databases can address its own records by **Primary Key** and address other tables by **Foreign Key**.

- Normalization rules insist that data must not be duplicated within a database, and column data types must be defined.

- Data integrity is preserved by database constraints.

- SQL Server is integrated with Visual Studio to allow databases to be created from within the IDE.

- Table constraints are established in the **Table Definition**.

- Setting the **Primary Key** column's **Is Identity** property to **True** will automatically number each row.

- Foreign keys can be created by the **Add New Foreign Key** option of the **Foreign Keys** item in the **Table Definition**.

- New **Foreign Key** constraints must be edited to describe the parent-child relationship between two tables.

- Table constraints are tested in real-time as **Table Data** is input.

- A database **Dataset** is an in-memory representation of the data contained within the database tables.

- Drag and drop a table from the **Data Sources** window onto a Form to automatically create data controls.

- A **BindingSource** manages the data flow between a **Dataset** and Form controls.

- Drag and drop a table from the **Data Sources** window onto a control to bind meaningful data from the table to that control.

- A **TableAdapter** has methods to supply data to Form controls, and can add custom SQL queries to exploit the true power of databases by selecting specific data.

Index

G

J

K

H

L

I